Super Cheap Norway Travel Guide

For Elowen

Our Mission

Did you know you can fly on a private jet for $500? Yes, a fully private jet. Complete with flutes of champagne and reclinable creamy leather seats. Your average billionaire spends $20,00 on the exact same flight. You can get it for $500 when you book private jet empty leg flights. Amazed? Don't be. This is just one of thousands of ways you can travel luxuriously on a budget.

When our brain hears the word "budget" it hears deprivation, suffering, agony, even depression. But budget travel need not be synonymous with hostels and pack lunches. You can enjoy an incredible trip to Norway on a budget, just like you can enjoy a private jet flight for 10% of the normal cost when you know how. The past years have shown us travel is a gift we must cherish. We believe strongly that this gift is best enjoyed on a budget. Together with thrifty locals, we have funneled our passion for travel bargains into Super Cheap Norway.

Our passion is finding travel bargains. This doesn't mean doing less or sleeping exclusively in hostels. Someone who spends A LOT on travel hasn't planned or wants to spend their money. We promise you that with a bit of planning, you can experience a luxury trip to Norway on a budget.

Traveling need not be expensive; Travel guides, Travel agents, Travel bloggers and influencers often show you overpriced accommodation, restaurants and big-ticket attractions because they earn commission from your "we're on vacation" mentality, which often leads to reckless spending. Our mission is to teach you how to enjoy more for less and get the best value from every dollar you spend in Norway.

Taking a trip to Norway is not just an outer journey, it's an inner one. Budget travel brings you closer to locals, culture and authenticity; which makes your inner journey more fulfilling.

Super Cheap Norway will save you 1000 times what you paid for it while teaching you local tips and tricks. We have formulated a system to pass on to you, so you can enjoy a trip to Norway without the nightmare credit card bill.

Our mission is to dispel myths, save you tons of money, give you the local tips and tricks and help you find experiences in Norway that will flash before your eyes when you come to take your last breath on this beautiful earth.

Who this book is for and why anyone can enjoy budget travel

There is a big difference between being cheap and frugal. Who doesn't like to spend money on beautiful experiences?

Over 25 years of travel has taught me I could have a 20 cent experience that will stir my soul more than a $100 one. Of course, sometimes the reverse is true, my point is, spending money on travel is the best investment you can make but it doesn't have to be at levels set by hotels and attractions with massive ad spends and influencers who are paid small fortunes to get you to buy into something you could have for a fraction of the cost.

This book is for those who want to have the cold hard budget busting facts to hand (which is why we've included so many one page charts, which you can use as a quick reference), but otherwise, the book provides plenty of tips to help you shape your own Norway experience.

We have designed these travel guides to give you a unique planning tool to experience an unforgettable trip without spending the ascribed tourist budget.

This guide focuses on Norway's unbelievable bargains. Of course, there is little value in traveling to Norway and not experiencing everything it has to offer. Where possible, we've included cheap workarounds or listed the experience in the Loved but Costly sections.

When it comes to FUN budget travel, it's all about what you know. You can have all the feels without most of the bills. A few days spent planning can save you thousands. Luckily, we've done the planning for you, so you can distill the information in minutes not days, leaving you to focus on what matters: immersing yourself in the sights, sounds and smells of Norway, meeting awesome new people and feeling relaxed and happy. I sincerely hope our tips will bring you great joy at a fraction of the price you expected.

So, grab a cup of tea or coffee, put your feet up and relax; you're about to enter the world of enjoying Norway on the cheap. Oh, and don't forget a biscuit. You need energy to plan a trip of a lifetime on a budget.

Redefining Super Cheap

The value you get out of Super Cheap Norway is not based on what you paid for it; it's based on what you do with it. You can only do great things with it if you believe saving money is worth your time. Charging things to your credit card and thinking 'oh I'll pay it off when I get home' is something you won't be tempted to do if you change your beliefs now. Think about what you associate with the word cheap, because you make your beliefs and your beliefs make you.

I grew up thinking you had to spend more than you could afford to have a good time traveling. Now I've visited 190 countries, I know nothing is further from the truth. Before you embark upon reading our specific tips for Norway think about your associations with the word cheap.

Here are the dictionary definitions of cheap:

- Costing very little; relatively low in price; inexpensive: a cheap dress.
- costing little labor or trouble: Words are cheap.
- charging low prices: a very cheap store.
- Of little account; of small value; mean; shoddy: Cheap conduct; cheap workmanship.
- Embarrassed; sheepish: He felt cheap about his mistake.
- Stingy; miserly: He's too cheap to buy his own brother a cup of coffee.

Three out of six definitions have extremely negative connotations. The 'super cheap' we're talking about in this book is not shoddy, embarrassed, or stingy.
We added the super to reinforce our message. Super's dictionary definition stands for 'a super quality'. Super Cheap

stands for enjoying the best on the lowest budget. Question other people's definitions of cheap so you're not blinded to possibilities, potential, and prosperity. Here are some new associations to consider forging:

Shoddy

Cheap stuff doesn't last is an adage marketing companies have drilled into consumers. However, by asking vendors the right questions cheap doesn't mean something won't last. I had a $10 backpack last for 8 years and a $100 suitcase bust on the first journey.

A study out of San Francisco University found that people who spent money on experiences rather than things were happier. Memories last forever, not things, even expensive things. And as we will show you during this guide, you don't need to pay to create glorious memories.[1]

Embarrassed

I have friends who routinely pay more to vendors because they think their money is putting food on this person's table. Paradoxically, Cuban doctors are driving taxis because they earn more money; it's not always a good thing for the place you're visiting to pay more and can cause unwanted distortion in their culture - Airbnb pushing out renters is an obvious example. Think carefully about whether the extra money is helping people or incentivising greed.

Stingy

---

[1]   Paulina Pchelin & Ryan T. Howell (2014) The hidden cost of value-seeking: People do not accurately forecast the economic benefits of experiential purchases, The Journal of Positive
Psychology, 9:4, 322-334, DOI: 10.1080/17439760.2014.898316

Cheap can be eco-friendly. Buying thrift clothes is cheap, but you also help the Earth. Many travellers are often disillusioned by the reality of traveling since the places on our bucket-lists are overcrowded. Cheap can take you away from the crowds. You can find balance and harmony being cheap. "Remember a journey is best measured in friends, rather than miles." – Tim Cahill. And making friends is free!

A recent survey by Credit Karma found 50% of Millennials and Gen Z get into debt traveling. **Please don't allow credit card debt to be an unwanted souvenir you take home.** As you will see from this book, there's so much you can enjoy in Norway for free, some many unique bargains and so many ways to save money! You just need to want to!

Discover Norway

Loften Islands

Norway is an ultimate bucket list destination; Breathtakingly beautiful fjords, mountains, unmatched wildlife, outstanding natural and historical heritage make two weeks of exploration fly.

Norway has the reputation of being among the most expensive destinations in the world. Norway is a land of prosperity, with the average monthly salary being 4500 USD. Fortunately, some of the best things in life are free (or almost free). This guides will show you how you can stretch your budget to experience Norway's amazing scenery, the midnight sun, the northern lights and the seemingly endless coastline with its charming towns and majestic fjords on just $250 for two weeks.

Norway is rich in history. The Norwegian land emerged from the last Ice Age. The oldest human skeleton found in Norway is carbon dated to 6,600 BC. The vikings represent Norways most famous civilisation. In the 8th century they are first recorded invading a seaside village in England. They left an indelible mark not just on Norway but across Europe and further. Modern day Norway, as we see it today has only existed for 200 years.

Norwegian people take great pride in their mythology. The average people aren't especially interested in the Viking period but Norse Mythology heavily influences culture. Norwegians are happy to be Norwegian and they're proud of the country they've made. You'll see a lot of Norwegian flags flying around. The society is very family friendly despite a high divorce rate. Being a parent in Norway doesn't seem to be in conflict with being anything else.

Norwegian People
Norwegians have a reputation for being stand-offish and difficult to approach for foreigners. Their motto is 'Deeds, not words'. Norway is a sparsely populated country, 5 million people and 16 inhabitants per km2. Norwegians are reserved people in general but they are friendly and will help you when you ask. Norwegians are shaped by surviving a harsh climate more than war and social hierarchy, and you'll find them to be friendly, but stubborn and fiercely individualistic. Norway has become rather liberal in moral issues and thus similar to neighbours like Denmark and Sweden. Bottomline: they are polite and will always help you.

How to make friends with the Norwegians
As they say in Norway - let's call the shovel a shovel. Norwegians, similar to most northern people, are very reserved. Most believe Norway is the best country in the world. If you concur with this and have the opportunity to engage with Norwegians on-purpose you will definitely make friends. Just don't expect to strike up conversations with locals at the bus stop. As long as you've got an "in", like being at the same party or dinner the reservedness is not a problem.

What Makes Norway Special?

- Amongst its most distinctive features is the country's unique weather. It experiences a long, hard winter (November to March) with temperatures reaching -51!

- Norway's geography and extreme climate affects the country's culture. The Norwegians are particularly fond of the outdoors. They love skiing, and have won the most Winter Olympic medals in history.

- The country is also home to a unique indigenous people called the Sami. The Sami are indigenous herders of reindeer in the Arctic Circle. They have been herding reindeer in Norway since thousands of years. Their language is similar to Finno-Hungarian. There are about 40,000 Samis, who are part of Norway's indigenous population. They have their own flag, which features a circular sun symbol.

- Norwegians are proud of their humanitarianism. They are committed to saving the environment and protecting the land. Norway has a target of eliminating the sale of diesel and gasoline by 2025.

>You can always get help.
>If you're ill, going to the hospital is free (for the most part), and the government will pay your salary.
>If you can't work for some reason, you'll get enough money to get by.
>If you just gave birth, you (and your partner) will get paid parental leave for 42 weeks!

>If you go to prison, they'll focus on making sure that when you get out, you'll have the best life possible. And you'll get internet in your cell.
>University is free (unless they're private), you will have to pay for your books and supplies, and housing if you need somewhere to live, but the government will give you hand outs.

Some of Norway's Best Bargains

Get 70% off a Cruise

An average cruise can set you back $4,000. If you dream of cruising the oceans or Fjords, but find the pricing too high, look at **repositioning cruises**. You can save as much as 70% by taking a cruise which takes the boat back to its home port.

These one-way itineraries take place during low cruise seasons when ships have to reposition themselves to locations where there's warmer weather.

To find a repositioning cruise, go to vacationstogo.com/repositioning_cruises.cfm. This simple and often over-looked booking trick is great for avoiding long flights with children and can save you so much money!

It's worth noting we don't have any affiliations with any travel service or provider. The links we suggest are chosen based on our experience of finding the best deals.

Super Cheap Accommodation

If you're traveling in winter you'll find the cheapest accommodation in Norway are "hytte" cabins. You can find them on booking.com and finn.no starting at 200NOK a night.

DNT cabins are dotted along hiking and skiing trails and a perfect cheap stay. If you plan to visit the unmanned DNT cabins you'll need to become a member of DNT. https://english.dnt.no/routes-and-cabins/

PRO TIP: If you visit the Lofoten islands you'll find fisherman's cabins called Rorbuer to be the cheapest accommodation.

Ride the Flamsbana railway

Flamsbana is the steepest in the world. This scenic route through the mountainous fjords and valleys of Southern Norway is considered one of the most beautiful train journeys in the world. It's a 20 kilometre train ride that takes around 40 minutes to complete. On the ride, you'll have incredible views of the fjords. The ride takes about an hour. Throughout the train passes through a number of tunnels that are among the most daring engineering feats in Norwegian history. 'The Flåm Railway, or Flåmsbana in Norwegian, goes from Flåm to Myrdal in Aurland, Norway. Boarding the train in Flåm is the most convenient way to take a trip.' Round-trip tickets are $45.

A super cheap alternative to this attraction is the Floyen funicular, which rises 425 meters above Bergen and costs just $4!

CHEAP CRUISE TIP: From Flam you can take a boat trip on the Naeroyfjord. The Naeroyfjord is a scenic journey that lasts approximately two hours and ends in the historic village of Gudvangen. Tickets cost NOK 540.00 $54.

Cheap Transport

Pre-Book Minipris Tickets

Buy your train tickets in advance. Purchasing minipris tickets can take 80% off your train travel! https://www.acprail.com/train-tickets/vy-minipris/

Buses

If you don't get minipris tickets travel by bus. Although less scenic buses are much cheaper than trains. The state-owned Vy is the main provider of long-distance bus services, while private outfits such as Nor-Way Bussekspress and Lavprisekspress also provide inexpensive buses. You can buy tickets in advance or pay on board.

EURAIL Scandinavia Pass

'The Eurail Scandinavia Pass lets you explore Denmark, Norway, Sweden and Finland by train' If you intend to travel a lot by train in these countries, it can save you a considerable amount of money. Check the options to see if its right for you. https://www.eurail.com/en/eurail-passes/one-country-pass/scandinavia

SAVE A FORTUNE ON
Renting a car

getaround.no works exactly the same way as Airbnb but for cars. You can save 1000% on your car rental by using this instead of Enterprise or other car rental services. Visit getaround.no to look at cars available during your stay.

If you're driving make sure to compare gas prices. They can differ wildly in the same town. GasBuddy is one of the best apps to maximize your gas savings.

PRO TIP: Nearly all ferries in Norway are cheaper before 9am for vehicles. If you're driving you can avoid the toll roads ($54 per toll!) and use ferry crossings cheaply before 9am.

Take advantage of Fisherman's Paradise

The country is home to 400 salmon-bearing rivers and there are over 65,000 lakes in Norway. You are welcome to fish totally for free in the incredible Norwegian sea and Fjord saltwaters, provided that you use hand held tackle only. (It is prohibited to fish species that you can only catch legally with other gear than handheld tackle.) and it is illegal to sell your catch. You'll find many well-stocked tackle shops near to seas and Fjords. You can catch Cod, Flounder, Haddock, Mackerel, Halibut and more. A mere sliver of these fishes would set you back at least $10 in Norway so catching a whole fish is a great way to enjoy delicious fish in Norway practically for free.

Here are some of Norway's best fishing spots:

Hardangervidda
Located in south-central Norway, Hardangervidda is an idyllic destination for outdoor adventures. It is a vast plateau with many lakes, rivers and glaciers. The area is also home to the largest herd of wild reindeer in Europe.

Flatanger region
Fishing in Flatanger is excellent year-round. The area is a good source for cod, ling, coalfish, and halibut. Fish stocks are especially high in winter, spring, and summer.

Lake Mjosa
Located 56 km north of Oslo, Lake Mjosa is the largest lake in Norway. It is one of Norway's best fishing spots. There are 20 species of fish found here.

Gjovik

The best fishing spots in Norway include the town of Gjovik, located around the largest lake in Norway, Lake Mjosa.

Go Mushroom picking

Norway is mushroom picking paradise. No one picks them here so its common to find them everywhere. Hedgehog mushrooms, chanterelles, trumpet chanterelles and ceps are all abundant, safe and healthy. Use an app like **Champignouf** to identify the species of a mushroom from a picture.

There are three edible mushrooms in Norway: boletes, chanterelle, and hedgehog. If you're a beginner, you'll find the hedgehog mushroom to be the easiest to find. These are often found in ditches and forests. A good way to identify these mushrooms is by their fruity smell.

One of the easiest places to pick mushrooms in Norway is in the forest.

If you plan on picking mushrooms in Norway, you should know about the **black trumpet mushroom**. This mushroom is very popular in the northern parts of the country. It is often considered mild and has a delicious taste. It is also considered slightly toxic when raw. **They should be cooked for 15 minutes or more BEFORE being eaten**.

PRO TIP: The cloudberry is an edible berry that can be found everywhere in Norway. It grows in marshlands, and has white flowers. It has a soft consistency and is full of vitamin C. The best way to pick cloudberries is to walk through marshes. They ripen in late July or August.

Find Supermarket Deals

Download the app "Mattilbud" for an update every week for which grocery store has what on sale.

Rema 1000
Rema 1000 is the cheapest supermarket in Norway. It's a no-frills, discount grocery chain that provides low prices on a variety of products. It's part of the Coop group, which is known all over Scandinavia.

How to Enjoy ALLO-CATING Money in Norway

'Money's greatest intrinsic value—and this can't be overstated—is its ability to give you control over your time.' - Morgan Housel

Notice I have titled the chapter how to enjoy allocating money in Norway. I'll use saving and allocating interchangeably in the book, but since most people associate saving to feel like a turtleneck, that's too tight, I've chosen to use wealth language. Rich people don't save. They allocate. What's the difference? Saving can feel like something you don't want or wish to do and allocating has your personal will attached to it.

And on that note, it would be helpful if you considered removing the following words and phrase from your vocabulary for planning and enjoying your Norway trip:

- Wish

- Want

- Maybe someday

These words are part of poverty language. Language is a dominant source of creation. Use it to your advantage. You don't have to wish, want or say maybe someday to Norway.

'People don't like to be sold-but they love to buy.' - Jeffrey Gitomer.

Every good salesperson who understands the quote above places obstacles in the way of their clients' buying. Companies create waiting lists, restaurants pay people to queue outside in order to create demand. People reason if something is so in demand, it must be worth having but that's often just marketing. Take this sales maxim 'People don't like to be sold-but they love to buy and flip it on its head to allocate your money in Norway on things YOU desire. You love to spend and hate to be sold. That means when something comes your way, it's not 'I can't afford it,' it's 'I don't want it' or maybe 'I don't want it right now'.

Saving money doesn't mean never buying a latte, never taking a taxi, never taking vacations (of course, you bought this book). Only you get to decide on how you spend and on what. Not an advice columnist who thinks you can buy a house if you never eat avocado toast again.

I love what Kate Northrup says about affording something: "If you really wanted it you would figure out a way to get it. If it were that VALUABLE to you, you would make it happen."

I believe if you master the art of allocating money to bargains, it can feel even better than spending it! Bold claim, I know. But here's the truth: Money gives you freedom and options. The more you keep in your account and or invested the more freedom and options you'll have. The principal reason you should save and allocate money is TO BE FREE! Remember, a trip's main purpose is relaxation, rest and enjoyment, aka to feel free.

When you talk to most people about saving money on vacation. They grimace. How awful they proclaim not to go wild on your vacation. If you can't get into a ton of debt enjoying your once-in-a-lifetime vacation, when can you?

When you spend money 'theres's a sudden rush of dopamine which vanishes once the transaction is complete.

What happens in the brain when you save money? It increases feelings of security and peace. You don't need to stress life's uncertainties. And having a greater sense of peace can actually help you save more money.' Stressed out people make impulsive financial choices, calm people don't.'

The secret to enjoying saving money on vacation is very simple: never save money from a position of lack. Don't think 'I wish I could afford that'. Choose not to be marketed to. Choose not to consume at a price others set. Don't save money from the flawed premise you don't have enough. Don't waste your time living in the box that society has created, which says saving money on vacation means sacrifice. It doesn't.

Traveling to Norway can be an expensive endeavor if you don't approach it with a plan, but you have this book which is packed with tips. The biggest other asset is your perspective.

OVERVIEW: How on earth am I going to travel Norway for $250 for two weeks?

Lofoten wild camping

While we will go through every bargain individually in the guide there are some underlying principles for a super cheap trip to Norway: FREE wild camping, cheap local transport and cheap supermarket food that is delicious.

Your flight into Oslo is not included in the budget (but from Poland, you can fly for $4 to Oslo - take the Polski bus from any European city to make it to the Warsaw, Krakow or Gdansk airports).

The first step to saving money is timing your trip. Go in July and August and wild camp (camping outside camp sites).

Norway is one of the only countries in the world where you can camp for free anywhere (as long as you are150m from a dwelling/ leave no trace/ stay max 2 nights). This alone can save you $4000 and is much easier and more enjoyable than you think.

One of the great advantages of Norway is that you don't have to cover huge distances to see Norway at its best because it is stunning absolutely everywhere and with the cheap train tickets you don't need to carry your pack and tent everywhere unless you want to.

Option One: Visit the Top Three Norwegian Cities + hostels

Oslo 6 days and nights

You land at Gardermoen airport and take the airport bus into Oslo city centre – Order online the same day and get your tickets for 125kr for adults, students/senior/child 65kr. (You save about 20-25kr per ticket by ordering online). Depending on the time you arrive, the local train can cost as little as $7 from the airport. Take the R10/R11 Regional Train or the L12 Local Train.

2 Nights accommodation in Anker Hostel - 155kr a night Activities in Oslo within walking distance (some taken from our free things to do in Oslo list). Take a walk down Karl Johan / City centre, Vigelandsparken, the national art gallery, Akershus fastening (national defence museum), Aker bridge (pier) and the Opera building. All these activities are free. Bus/tram/metro/ferry 24 hour pass: 80kr

Food and drinks: The hostel has a kitchen, so all meals in our budget except one are made in the apartment with food bought from grocery stores. 3 meals per day, 2x breakfast, 1x dinner, 2x evening meals. Groceries for simple spaghetti bolognese for 2 people: 80kr, 2 bread, cheese, ham, pesto (another condiment): 180kr Eating out once: Café Elias Mat og Sånt (offers traditional Norwegian food): 2 mains and 2 non-alcoholic drinks: 500kr Two visits to local cafes: 4x coffee/tee: 120kr Sum Oslo: 2520kr (1260 per person)

2. Bergen 4 days and nights

Transportation by train from Oslo to Bergen "Minipris": 149kr per person. You arrive by train in the City centre and will have no need for transportation during your stay Accommodation: Marken Gjestehus (read more here) 210kr (per person per day in a dorm): 840kr Activities (some from the free things to do in Bergen list): Visit the UNESCO site Hanseatic Warf at the Bergen pier,

Walk around Sandviken and Nordnes, take the funicular up to Fløyen (40kr per person) and walk down or walk from Fløyen to Ulrikken and take the tramway down from Ulrikken (80kr per person, includes bus back to city center). Food and drinks: Groceries for breakfast and evening meals: 200kr. Eating out, dinner for two days: Naboen (basement) Restaurant (Norwegian food) and Zupperia Restaurant: About 700kr total. Eating out, lunch one day: Søstrene Hagelin (Fish soup, Bergen speciality): About 100kr
Sum Bergen: 2578kr (1289kr per person)

3. Stavanger 4 days and nights
Transportation by bus from Bergen to Stavanger: 369kr per person (Nettbus.no).
Accommodation: Hostel Stavanger, centrally located apartment: 242kr per night.
Activities: Pulpit Rock.
Bus + Ferry roundtrip: 250kr per person. (whole day trip, 4hour hike) Activities: Walk around in the city centre, old Stavanger and visit Domkirke (Cathedral):
Food and drinks: Groceries for breakfast and evening meals + 1 dinner: 300kr Eating out, dinner one day: Cafe Sting Restaurant: About 350kr for two persons Flight from Stavanger to Oslo one way: About 300kr per person Sum Stavanger and Oslo flight: 3372kr (1686kr per person)
Total cost for 2 weeks in Norway, visiting three cities: $250 per person.

Option Two (our preferred route) Head North and Wild Camp in July/August

In Norway, due to a law called allemannsretten (pronounced ALL-eh-mahns-ret-en) you can camp for free as long as you are 150m from a dwelling. And leave no trace and stay a maximum of 2 nights.

Packing List for two weeks camping in Norway (you want to pack as light as possible - lend things if you cannot afford to buy and check thrift shops before buying anything new) Rucksack: Golite Jam. Boots: Demon Ultralight, Sandals: Source X-Strap. Sleeping System: Arete Marmot Down bag, Thermarest Prolite 3 Short. Clothes: Trekmates long sleeved base layer, Craghoppers Wicking T-Shirt, Go-lite sleeveless T-shirt, Running shorts, Trekmates Pertex Windshirt, Helly Hanson polyamide walking trousers, 3 pairs socks (threw away and bought more as we went). 3 pairs briefs, 1 sports crop top, Craghoppers Intelligent Response insulated jacket, homemade Pertex pinafore dress! Waterproofs: Outdoor Scene Mini Pac Jacket and Trousers. Trekmates waterproof broad brimmed hat. Hydration: 2x1 litre aluminium bottles. Cook Kit: Coleman F1 Ultralite gas stove, gas bottle, steel saucepan, 2xTitanium Sporks. Opinel knife. Lighter x2. Wash kit: 2x tooth brush, Weleda salt toothpaste, 1/2 bar soap, toilet roll, 12" square magic towel, tiny hairbrush. Miscellaneous: Tin Mug. Vitamin pills, cockle pendant, glasses case, Mosquito head net. Organic Tea Bags as a secret treat.

Total Pack Weight: About 6 Kilos plus water (pack weight is the weight of all of above minus boots and minimal clothes).

The Route OSLO - 2 DAYS

Land in Oslo (main airport) buy the train ticket to the city ahead of time for 30kr. Stay at Anker Hostel 2 days Follow all our free things to do in Oslo Eat meals at the hostel, buy budget own.
Take the train to Oppdal (145kr)

HIKE OPPDAL TO TRONDHEIM 3 DAYS

Buy food ahead of time Wild camp near the Høgvang-parken Park. Walk the St Olaf's trial to Trondheim Wild camp and cook using camping stove away. Ensure you have enough food for 3 days for the walk to Trondheim.

Trondheim 1 DAY Arrive

Recharge batteries at Airbnb $20 a night - https://www.airbnb.com/rooms/734767729366140187

Travel to Lofoten Islands 7 DAYS (the most beautiful place in Norway - in my opinion)

Public transport may be cheaper than driving, expect if you use blablacar.com (ride sharing in Norway). Express boat Svolvær-Bodø is NOK 333 pp (www.torghatten-Nord.no/English/default-.aspx), train Bodø-Trondheim, tickets at NOK 199 when booked at http://www.nsb.no/ exactly 90 days in advance. Driving time is around 12-13hrs. on E6 with ferry Svolvær-Skutvik. However, if you choose to drive, the coastal highway 17 is much more scenic, will require 3 days. Once you arrive at Lofoten there will be many wild camping spots. You will experience landscapes teeming with shimmering fjords, rugged mountains, quiant fishing villages forgotten by time and picturesque valleys

Getting home: You can take the overnight train back to Oslo for a super cheap flight. Or take a flight from Lofoten's nearest airport, Bodo.

Deviate from our route by adding: Rjukan Rjukan is perfect for shorter trips from Oslo, with a fascinating WWII history and what I think is Norway's most beautiful mountain: Gaustatoppen. Rjukan has recently made huge efforts to expand parking areas, so this is one of the few places in Norway that is actively trying to draw in more visitors. You will be really welcome here! Åna-Sira Here you can also hike up Brufjell, which is famous for Ice Age potholes that look out over the sea or relax by the beach.

Mandal is Norway's southernmost town and while it's not exactly a hidden gem, it's nowhere near as crowded as the fjords in the summer. The town itself has colourful wooden houses along the water and a cute little centre with cobblestone streets and a beautiful beach: Sjøsanden.

The Most Beautiful Accessible Fjords in Norway

You don't necessarily need an expensive cruise to explore Norway's Fjords. You can kayak, bike around them or just simply stand and take in there magnificent beauty for free. Here are the best to consider visiting:

Hardangerfjord (Bergen)

Hardangerfjord is one of the longest fjords in Norway. This fjord begins from the Atlantic Ocean and ends in Odda. It is known for its pristine waters, abundant fruit trees, and scenic hiking trails. You will also find small charming villages, world-class fishing, and beautiful national parks. The Hardangerfjord has become a popular domestic tourism destination. In addition to its stunning beauty, it's home to numerous waterfalls and glaciers.

During springtime, you can expect cherry blossoms and colorful gardens along the fjord. You will also find beautiful villages and small towns. You can reach it easily and cheaply by the 740 bus from Bergen (but check the timetable as it runs ONLY 5 times a week).

In addition to its natural beauty, Hardanger offers a wide variety of cultural experiences. There is a Folk Museum in Utne that displays traditional embroidery and costumes. Tickets cost NOK 115.

Lysefjord

Lysefjorden is known for its sweeping views of the surrounding mountains. There are many hiking trails, which are closed in the winter. In summer, there are guided kayak trips that take guests into caves and around waterfalls. Lysefjorden is home to Preikestolen, which is a 604-metre-high cliff. This towering rock offers amazing views of the Lysefjord. There are also fjord sightseeing tours available.

Located in Rogaland county in southwest Norway, Lysefjord is a long, narrow fjord. It measures 42 kilometers from its head to its end. The fjord has a depth of more than 400 metres. The cheapest way to Lysefjord is the express ferry, fare 141 NOK one way from Stavanger.

Geirangerfjord

The Geirangerfjord is one of the most spectacular fjords in Norway. It has been designated as a UNESCO World Heritage Site. It is a place of great natural beauty with towering mountain peaks and several waterfalls. The cheapest way to get to Geiranger is to travel from Ålesund by ferry and bus line 211 which costs NOK 260 and takes 5 hours.

Aurlandsfjord

Aurlandsfjord is a narrow offshoot of Sognefjorden and a breathtaking fjord. Flam is located at the southern end of Aurlandsfjord. It's a great base to explore the surrounding area. Bus line NW420 from Flam costs $3 and take 30 minutes to reach Aurlandsfjord.

Naeroyfjord

The fjord is surrounded by majestic mountains that soar to over a thousand metres in height. The landscape is also dotted with waterfalls, small hamlets, and hanging valleys. The area is best explored by car but you can also take a ferry from Flam to reach Naeroyfjord.

Best Accessible Waterfalls in Norway

Norway is home to a staggering 300 + waterfalls. Watching water cascade from the mountains is an unmissable experience in Norway and its FREE!

Steinsdalsfossen

One of the best waterfalls in Norway is the Steinsdalsfossen, a 46 meter high cascade that cascades over a narrow ledge into a river valley. You can go behind this waterfall. The best time to visit is early summer when the snow melts off the mountains and finds its way down the fjord. You can reach the waterfall from Bergen on the 930 bus. The journey takes 1.5 hours.

Latefossen

The Oddadalen Valley has seven waterfalls over a distance of 10 km. The road that connects Odda to Haugesund passes right by the falls. The area is known for its scenic rides and spectacular viewpoints of Hardangerfjord.

You can reach the waterfall from Bergen on the 930 bus. The journey takes 3 hours.

Vinnufossen

The sixth highest waterfall in the world. The water of this waterfall cascades down in four stages, resulting in a total drop of 860 meters. The waterfall is part of the Vinnu River, which is fed by the Vinnufonna glacier. The glacier is the largest glacier in More and Romsdal counties. The best time to visit is in summer, although the waterfall is also beautiful in spring.

You can reach the waterfall from Trondheim with bus and train. The journey takes 3 hours.

Kjosfossen

Kjosfossen is one of the largest in the country. It is also one of the most popular tourist attractions in Norway. The Kjosfossen waterfall is located in the county of Sogn og Fjordane, near the town of Myrdal.

Kjosfossen is a waterfall that falls 225 meters. It is a part of the Flam Line railway.

Kjosfossen is only accessible by train. In fact, you can snap a photo of the waterfall from the train platform. You should be on the right side of the train to see the waterfall properly. **You need to purchase the train tickets in advance as tickets are usually sold out during the summer. The train from Mydral costs $2 and takes 10 minutes.**

NOTE: Trains do not stop at Kjosfossen during the winter season.

Best Off-the-beaten track in Norway

We will explore the major destinations and how to enjoy each on the super cheap but here are some smaller towns you might want to consider visiting:

Bodo

Bodo is the northernmost city on the national railway system in Norway and a major trade and transport hub. The city also serves as the main gateway to the Lofoten Islands.

Bodo is a town surrounded by impressive mountain backdrops. This makes Bodo a great jumping off point for adventurers. It also has a lively aviation sports community.
You can take a ferry to the Lofoten Islands from Bodo. The Lofoten Islands are a popular scenic destination in Norway.

The ferry trip takes about half an hour and the ride is very scenic and costs $25.

There are 17 nature reserves in the Bodo area and plenty of breathtaking hikes. Bodo is also home to the Norsk Luftfartsmuseum. The museum is located on the site of a former German airport during World War II. There are many exhibits to explore including a U2 spy plane and a flight simulator.

Haugesund

The town is nestled between the brisk North Sea and rocky mountains. This charming town is known for its historic connection to the sea. The main street in Haugesund is lined with cafes and shops and there are plenty of incredible hikes nearby. The Dokken Museum is open in the summer, and features several buildings that tell the story of the herring industry. Herring is a beloved national dish and you'll find locals enjoying it pickled and zesty.

Arendal

Arendal is a small port city which has a picturesque look. It is surrounded by mountains of up to 6,000 feet and is located on the Romsalsfjord. The town centre is made of wooden houses dating back to the 17th century and Trinity Church is awe-inspiring.

Moskenes

Moskenes is part of the Lofoten archipelago. The archipelago is known for its scenic landscape, fishing industry, and diverse wildlife. The best time to visit Lofoten is between June and August. You'll find a beautiful landscape of jagged peaks, well-preserved fishing village and historic buildings.

Henningsvaer

Also located on the Lofoten Islands, Henningsvaer is a great town to visit for its unique atmosphere and history. It is a fishing village that has been converted into a tourist resort, but that does not mean that it has lost its character. Its beautiful harbor, colorful docks and narrow streets are beautiful.

Henningsvaer is known for its many art galleries and shops. Some of the best places to visit include the Kaviar Factory, the Museum of Photography, and the Lofoten Art Gallery.

Planning your trip

When to visit?

Norway is gorgeous in all seasons, but If you are not tied to school holidays, the best time to visit is during the shoulder-season months of late spring or early Fall - May and September.

The Mela music festival is the countries largest music festival, it's **free** and held annually in August. Find the details here: https://www.mela.no/en/

May 17th is Norway's national day. If you visit then you'll be greeted by a huge parade in Oslo and the King and Queen waving from the Palace balcony.

Christmas in Norway is unforgettable, but expect crowds and high prices. Plus you can't wild camp. If you want to visit Norway for the Christmas markets, your best bet would be to visit in late November when the Christmas markets start but the crowds haven't arrived.

How to be a green tourist in Norway

There is a bizarre misconception that you have to spend money to travel in an eco-friendly way. This like, all marketing myths was concocted and hyped by companies seeking to make money off of you. In my experience, anything with eco in front of their names e.g Eco-tours will be triple the cost of the regular tour.

Sometimes its best to take these tours if you're visiting endangered areas, but normally such places have extensive legislation that everyone, including the eco and noneco tour companies, are complying with. The vast majority of ways you can travel eco-friendly are free and even save you money.

Avoid Bottled Water - get a good water bottle and refill. The water in Norway is safe to drink and delicious.
Thrift shop but check the labels and don't buy polyester clothes - overtime plastic is released into the ocean when we wash polyester.
Don't put it in a plastic bag, bring a cotton tote with you when you venture out.
Pack Light - this is one of the best ways to save money. If you find a 5-star hotel for tonight for $10, and you're at an Airbnb or hostel, you can easily pack and upgrade hassle free. A light pack equals freedom and it means less to wash.
Travel around Norway on Bikes or e-Scooters or use Public Transportation.
Car Pool with services like bla bla car or Uber/Lyft share.
Walk, this is the best way to get to know Norway. You never know what's around the corner.
Travel Overland - this isn't always viable especially if you only have limited time off work, but where possible avoid flying and if you have to compensate by off-setting or keeping the rest of your trip carbon-neutral by doing all of the above.

Saving money on Food

Eat Taco's

Compared to other Nordic countries, Norwegian food is relatively expensive with one notable and slightly odd exception, Mexican food in Norway is quite a bargain. Tacos can be found cheaply in every grocery store in Norway.

Use 'Too Good To Go'

Oslo offers plenty of food bargains; if you know where to look. Thankfully the app 'Too Good to Go' is turning visitors into locals by showing them exactly where to look. In Oslo you can pick up a $15 buy of baked goods for $2.99. You'll find lots of fish dishes on offer in Oslo, which would normally be expensive.

How it works? You pay for a magic bag on the app and simply pick it up from the bakery or restaurant during the time they've selected. You can find extremely cheap breakfast, lunch, dinner and even groceries this way. Simply download the app and press 'my current location' to find the deals near you in Oslo. .What's not to love about cheap, delicious food and helping drive down food waste? It's worth nothing this works in Bregen and Trondheim but not outside the cities.

An oft-quoted parable is 'There is no such thing as cheap food. Either you pay at the cash registry or the doctor's office'. This dismisses the fact that good nutrition is a choice; we all make every-time we eat. Cheap eats are not confined to hotdogs and kebabs. The great thing about using Too Good To Go is you can eat nutritious food cheaply: fruits, vegetables, fish and nut dishes are a fraction of their supermarket cost.

Japan has the longest life expectancy in the world. A national study by the Japanese Ministry of Internal Affairs and Communications revealed that between January and May 2019, a household of two spent on average ¥65,994 a month, that's $10 per person per day on food. You truly don't need to spend a lot to eat nutritious food. That's a marketing gimmick hawkers of overpriced muesli bars want you to believe.

Never pick up a bag with a rating lower than 4.2 on the Too Good To Go app. People using it tend to be kinder because its fighting food waster.

Oft for dagens rätt midweek menu's

They cost 50-100 NOK and include a drink, salad buffet, bread, and coffee. It's literally half the price of what you'd pay at dinner. San Francisco Bread Bowl has a good dagens menu in Oslo.

Eat at golf courses
Weirdly the are some of the better restaurants in Norway, especially when traveling along motorways. Look out for the golf sign and names followed by the abbreviation GK (golf club).

Breakfast
If you stay somewhere with a free breakfast, eat smart. Don't eat sugary cereals or white flour rich pastries if you don't want to be hungry an hour later. Before leaving your hotel or checking out, find some fresh fruit, water, and granola in the fitness centre or coffee in the lobby or business

centre. If your hotel doesn't have free breakfast, don't take it. You can always eat cheaper outside.

Backstube Solli Plass has the best cheap breakfast we found in Oslo. Here you can pick up a traditional Norwegian breakfast for less than $6!

Visit supermarkets at discount times.

You can get a 50 per cent discount around 5 pm at the Kiwi supermarkets on fresh produce. The cheaper the super-market, the less discounts you will find, so check Kiwi at 5pm rather than discount stores like the Rema. Some items are also marked down due to sell-by date after the lunchtime rush so its also worth to check in around 3 pm.

Use delivery services on the cheap

Take advantage of local offers on food delivery services. Most platforms including ubereats and Deliveroo offer $10 off the first order in Norway.

SNAPSHOT: How to enjoy a $5,000 trip to Norway for $250

(full breakdown at the end of the guide)

Stay	Travelling in peak season:
	1. Wild camp 2. Last-minute hotels via priceline.com express deals 3. Stay in a private room in a Airbnb if you want privacy and cooking facilities. 4. Stay in hostels if you want to meet over travellers. Travelling in low-season 1. Wild camp 2. Last minute five-star hotels.
Eat	Protein heavy fish specialities such as Smoked salmon. 'Too Good to Go' magic bags
Move	Train and public transport in cities. .t-bane pass for three days $18 or use the free city bikes. The Oslo Pass gives you free travel by bus, train, boat and tram in and around Oslo.
See	Fjords, mountains, swimming, hikes, museums, (on their free days)
Total	US$250

How to use this book

Google and TripAdvisor are your on-the-go guides while traveling, a travel guide adds the most value during the planning phase, and if you're without Wi-Fi. Always download the google map for your destination - having an offline map will make using this guide much more comfortable. For ease of use, we've set the book out the way you travel, booking your flights, arriving, how to get around, then on to the money-saving tips. The tips we ordered according to when you need to know the tip to save money, so free tours and combination tickets feature first. We prioritized the rest of the tips by how much money you can save and then by how likely it was that you could find the tip with a google search. Meaning those we think you could find alone are nearer the bottom. I hope you find this layout useful. If you have any ideas about making Super Cheap Insider Guides easier to use, please email me philgattang@gmail.com

A quick note on How We Source Super Cheap Tips
We focus entirely on finding the best bargains. We give each of our collaborators $2,000 to hunt down never-before-seen deals. The type you either only know if you're local or by on the ground research. We spend zero on marketing and a little on designing an excellent cover. We do this yearly, which means we just keep finding more amazing ways for you to have the same experience for less.

Now let's get started with juicing the most pleasure from your trip to Norway with the least possible money!

OUR SUPER CHEAP TIPS...

Here are our specific tips to to enjoy a $5,000 trip to Norway for $250

How to Find Super Cheap Flights to Norway

Luck is just an illusion. Anyone can find incredible flight deals. If you can be flexible you can save huge amounts of money. In fact, the biggest tip I can give you for finding incredible flight deals is simple: find a flexible job. Don't despair if you can't do that theres still a lot you can do. The following pages detail the exact method I use to consistently find cheap flights to Norway.

Book your flight to Norway on a Tuesday or Wednesday

Tuesdays and Wednesdays are the cheapest days of the week to fly. You can take a flight to Norway on a Tuesday or Wednesday for less than half the price you'd pay on a Thursday Friday, Saturday, Sunday or Monday.

Start with Google Flights (but NEVER book through them)

I conduct upwards of 50 flight searches a day for readers. I use google flights first when looking for flights. I put specific departure but broad destination (e.g Europe) and usually find amazing deals.

The great thing about Google Flights is you can search by class. You can pick a specific destination and it will tell you which time is cheapest in which class. Or you can put in dates and you can see which area is cheapest to travel to.

But be aware Google flights does not show the cheapest prices among the flight search engines but it does offer several advantages

1. You can see the cheapest dates for the next 8 weeks. Other search engines will blackout over 70% of the prices.
2. You can put in multiple airports to fly from. Just use a common to separate in the from input.
3. If you're flexible on where you're going Google flights can show you the cheapest destinations.
4. You can set-up price tracking, where Google will email you when prices rise or decline.

Once you have established the cheapest dates to fly go over to skyscanner.net and put those dates in. You will find sky scanner offers the cheapest flights.

Get Alerts when Prices to Norway are Lowest

Google also has a nice feature which allows you to set up an alert to email you when prices to your destination are at their lowest. So if you don't have fixed dates this feature can save you a fortune.

Baggage add-ons

It may be cheaper and more convenient to send your luggage separately with a service like sendmybag.com Often the luggage sending fee is cheaper than what the airlines charge to check baggage. Visit Lugless.com or luggagefree.com in addition to sendmybag.com for a quotation.

Loading times

Anyone who has attempted to find a cheap flight will know the pain of excruciating long loading times. If you encounter this issue use google flights to find the cheapest dates and then go to skyscanner.net for the lowest price.

Always try to book direct with the airline

Once you have found the cheapest flight go direct to the airlines booking page. This is advantageous in the current covid cancellation climate, because if you need to change your flights or arrange a refund, its much easier to do so, than via a third party booking agent.

That said, sometimes the third party bookers offer cheaper deals than the airline, so you need to make the decision based on how likely you think it is that disruption will impede you making those flights.

More flight tricks and tips

www.secretflying.com/usa-deals offers a range of deals from the USA and other countries. For example you can pick-up a round trip flight non-stop from from the east coast to johannesburg for $350 return on this site

Scott's cheap flights, you can select your home airport and get emails on deals but you pay for an annual subscription. A free workaround is to download Hopper and set search alerts for trips/price drops.

Premium service of Scott's cheap flights.
They sometime have discounted business and first class but in my experience they are few and far between.

JGOOT.com has 5 times as many choices as Scott's cheap flights.

kiwi.com allows you to be able to do radius searches so you can find cheaper flights to general areas.

Finding Error Fares
Travel Pirates (www.travelpirates.com) is a gold-mine for finding error deals. Subscribe to their newsletter. I recently found a reader an airfare from Montreal-Brazil for a $200 round trip (mistake fare!). Of course these error fares are always certain dates, but if you can be flexible you can save a lot of money.

Things you can do that might reduce the fare to Norway:--
• Use a VPN (if the booker knows you booked one-way, the return fare will go up)
• Buy your ticket in a different currency

How to Find CHEAP FIRST-CLASS Flights to Norway

Upgrade at the airport

Airlines are extremely reluctant to advertise price drops in first or business class tickets so the best way to secure them is actually at the airport when airlines have no choice but to decrease prices dramatically because otherwise they lose money. Ask about upgrading to business or first-class when you check-in. If you check-in online look around the airport for your airlines branded bidding system. For example KLM at Amsterdam have terminals where you can bid on upgrades.

Use Air-miles

When it comes to accruing air-miles for American citizens **Chase Sapphire Reserve card** ranks top. If you put everything on there and pay it off immediately you will end up getting free flights all the time, aside from taxes.

Get 2-3 chase cards with sign up bonuses, you'll have 200k points in no time and can book with points on multiple airlines when transferring your points to them.

Please note, this is only applicable to those living in the USA. In the Bonus Section we have detailed the best air-mile credit cards for those living in the UK, Canada, Germany, Austria, Spain and Australia.

Cheapest route to Norway from America

At the time of writing TAP AIR are flying direct for around $325 return out of NYC. Norse Atlantic Airways also have return flights for around $350.

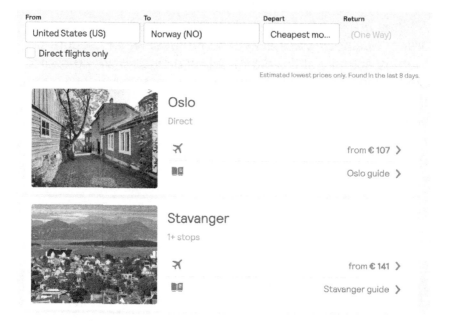

From	To	Depart	Return
United States (US)	Norway (NO)	Cheapest mo...	(One Way)

☐ Direct flights only

Estimated lowest prices only. Found in the last 8 days.

Oslo
Direct

✈   from € 107 ›

📖   Oslo guide ›

Stavanger
1+ stops

✈   from € 141 ›

📖   Stavanger guide ›

Arriving in Oslo

Oslo has three airports, the Oslo Airport Gardermoen (OSL), Sandefjord Airport, Torp (TRF) and Moss Airport, Rygge (RYG).

OSL, Gardermoen airport is closest to the city centre. It is the main international airport in Oslo and the one you should aim to arrive at.

The cheapest way from the Gardermoen airport is with train. Buy your ticket in advance at . This is always the cheapest form of travel if you book in advance. Even when you compare it to buses. Which are notoriously difficult to book and find.

NOTE: If you buy on arrival **do not buy a Flytoget ticket**. It's the same journey, 3 times the price.

INSIDER MONEY SAVING TIP

Don't fly Ryanair. They arrive at 'Oslo airport', 110km from Oslo. The bus or train to Oslo will cost you double your airfare. This is how cheap airlines get you.

Need a place to store luggage?
Use stasher.com to find a convenient place to store your luggage cheaply. It provides much cheaper options than airport and train station lockers in Norway.

PRO TIP: CHEAP COFFEE IN OSLO: Coffee at Joker is always $1. $5 everywhere else. https://joker.no/finn-butikk/joker-oslo-s

Cheapest Place to Stay in Oslo

The best price performance location in Oslo

A room putting Oslo's attractions, restaurants, and nightlife are within walking distance will save you time on transport but restaurants and bars get much cheaper the further you go from famous tourist attractions. You will also get a better idea of the day to day life of a local if you stay in a neighbourhood like Grønland. It depends on the Oslo you want to experience. For the tourist experience stay in the centre either in a last-minute hotel or Airbnb. For a taste of local life the leafy district of Grønland is the best you will find. Citybox Oslo is a luxurious threestar hotel with consistently rooms from $50 a night in the city. But again don't be scared to stay outside the centre, the public transport is relatively cheap, safe and fast.

The West End of Oslo offers a more quiet setting. The Old Town, also known as Gamlebyen, is a neighborhood in Oslo that dates back to the 11th century. It's home to cultural institutions and authentic Norwegian restaurants. It is one of the city's most beautiful neighborhoods.

If you want to party during your time in Oslo: Møllegata, Grünerløkka and Grønland offer the best nightlife scene in Oslo.

Hack your Oslo Accommodation

Use Time

There are two ways to use time. One is to book in advance. Three months will net you the best deal, especially if your visit coincides with an event. The other is to book on the day of your stay. This is a risky move, but if executed well, you can lay your head in a five-star hotel for a 2-star fee.

Before I travelled to Norway, I checked for big events using a simple google search 'What's on in Norway', there were no big events drawing travellers so I risked showing up with no accommodation booked (If there are big events on demand exceeds supply and you should avoid using this strategy) I started checking for discount rooms at 11 am using a private browser on booking.com.

Before I go into demand-based pricing, take a moment to think about your risk tolerance. By risk, I am not talking about personal safety. No amount of financial savings is worth risking that.

What I am talking about is being inconvenienced. Do you deal well with last-minute changes? Can you roll with the punches or do you dislike it if something changes? Everyone is different and knowing yourself is the best way to plan a great trip. If you are someone that likes to have everything pre-planned using demand-based pricing to get cheap accommodation will not work for you. Skip this section and go to blind-booking.

Demand-based pricing

Be they an Airbnb host or hotel manager; no one wants empty rooms. Most will do anything to make some revenue because they still have the same costs to cover whether the room is occupied or not. That's why you will find many hotels drastically slashing room rates for same-day bookings.

How to book five-star hotels for a two-star price

You will not be able to find these discounts when the demand exceeds the supply. So if you're visiting during the peak season, or during an event which has drawn many travellers don't try this.

On the day of your stay, visit booking.com (which offers better discounts than Kayak and agoda.com). Hotel Tonight individually checks for any last-minute bookings, but they take a big chunk of the action, so the better deals come from booking.com. The best results come from booking between 2 pm and 4 pm when the risk of losing any revenue with no occupancy is most pronounced, so algorithms supporting hotels slash prices. This is when you can find rates that are not within the "lowest publicly visible" rate. To avoid losing customers to other websites, or cheapening the image of their hotel most will only offer the super cheap rates during a two hour window from 2 pm to 4 pm. Two guests will pay 10x difference in price but it's absolutely vital to the hotel that neither knows it.

Takeaway: To get the lowest price book on the day of stay between 2 pm and 4 pm and extend your search radius to include further afield hotels with good transport connections.

How to trick travel Algorithms to get the lowest hotel price

Do not believe anyone who says changing your IP address to get cheaper hotels or flights does NOT work. If you don't believe us, download a Tor Network and search for flights and hotels to one destination using your current IP and then the tor network (a tor browser hits your IP address from algorithms. It is commonly used by hackers). You will receive different prices.

The price you see is a decision made by an algorithm that adjusts prices using data points such as past bookings, remaining capacity, average demand and the probability of selling the room or flight later at a higher price. If knows you've searched for the area before ip the prices high. To circumvent this, you can either use a different IP address from a cafe or airport or data from an international sim. I use a sim from Three, which provides free data in many countries around the world. When you search from a new IP address, most of the time, and particularly near booking you will get a lower price. Sometimes if your sim comes from a 'rich' country, say the UK or USA, you will see higher rates as the algorithm has learnt people from these countries pay more. The solution is to book from a local wifi connection - but a different one from the one you originally searched from.

How to get last-minute discounts on owner rented properties

In addition to Airbnb, you can also find owner rented rooms and apartments on www.vrbo.com or HomeAway or a host of others.

Nearly all owners renting accommodation will happily give renters a "last-minute" discount to avoid the space sitting empty, not earning a dime.

Go to Airbnb or another platform and put in today's date. Once you've found something you like start the negotiating by asking for a 25% reduction. A sample message to an Airbnb host might read:

Dear HOST NAME,

I love your apartment. It looks perfect for me. Unfortunately, I'm on a very tight budget. I hope you won't be offended, but I wanted to ask if you would be amenable to offering me a 25% discount for tonight, tomorrow and the following day? I see that you aren't booked. I can assure you, I will leave your place exactly the way I found it. I will put bed linen in the washer and ensure everything is clean for the next guest. I would be delighted to bring you a bottle of wine to thank you for any discount that you could offer.

If this sounds okay, please send me a custom offer, and I will book straight away.

YOUR NAME.

In my experience, a polite, genuine message like this, that proposes reciprocity will be successful 80% of the time. Don't ask for more than 25% off, this person still has to pay the bills and will probably say no as your stay will cost them more in bills than they make. Plus starting higher, can offend the owner and do you want to stay somewhere, where you have offended the host?

In Practice

To use either of these methods, you must travel light. Less stuff means greater mobility, everything is faster and you don't have to check-in or store luggage. If you have a lot of luggage, you're going to have fewer of these opportunities to save on accommodation. Plus travelling light benefits the planet - you're buying, consuming, and transporting less stuff.

Blind-booking

If your risk tolerance does not allow for last-minute booking, you can use blind-booking. Many hotels not wanting to cheapen their brand with known low-prices, choose to op-erate a blind booking policy. This is where you book without knowing the name of the hotel you're going to stay in until you've made the payment. This is also sometimes used as a marketing strategy where the hotel is seeking to recover from past issues. I've stayed in plenty of blind book hotels. As long as you choose 4 or 5 star hotels, you will find them to be clean, comfortable and safe. priceline.com, Hot Rate® Hotels and Top Secret Hotels (operated by last-minute.com) offer the best deals.

Hotels.com Loyalty Program

This is currently the best hotel loyalty program with hotels in Norway. The basic premise is you collect 10 nights and get 1 free. hotels.com price match, so if booking.com has a cheaper price you can get hotel.com, to match. If you intend to travel more than ten nights in a year, its a great choice to get the 11th free.

Don't let time use you.

Rigidity will cost you money. You pay the price you're willing to pay, not the amount it requires a hotel to deliver. Therefore if you're in town for a big event, saving money on accommodation is nearly impossible so in such cases book three months ahead.

TOP TIPS FOR BOOKING

- When searching online use the Norwerigan term for hostels vandrerhjem. You'll find more and cheaper.
- Visiting during summer vacation? Some Universities offer rooms during the summer. Search for college sovesaler + town.

Priceline Hack" to get a Luxury Hotel on the Cheap

While a luxury hotel isn't included in our two weeks for $250 they average around $400 a night in Norway but this Priceline hack can help you book one from $100.

Priceline.com has been around since 1997 and is an incredible site for sourcing luxury Hotels on the cheap in Norway. If you've tried everything else and that's failed, priceline will deliver.

Priceline have a database of the lowest price a hotel will accept for a particular time and date. That amount changes depending on two factors:

1. Demand: More demand high prices.
2. Likelihood of lost revenue: if the room is still available at 3pm the same-day prices will plummet.

Obviously they don't want you to know the lowest price as they make more commission the higher the price you pay.

They offer two good deals to entice you to book with them in Norway. And the good news is neither require last-minute booking (though the price will decrease the closer to the date you book).

'Firstly, 'price-breakers'. You blind book from a choice of three highly rated hotels which they name. Pricebreakers, travelers are shown three similar, highly-rated hotels, listed under a single low price.' After you book they reveal the

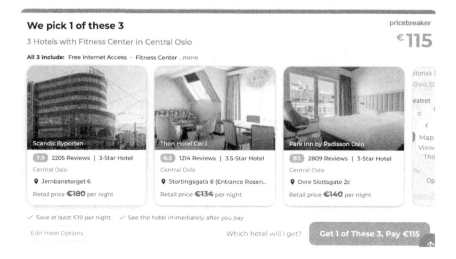

name of the hotel.

Secondly, the 'express deals'. These are the last minute deals. You'll be able to see the name of the hotel before you book.

To find the right luxury hotel for you at a cheap price you should plug in the
neighbourhoods you want to stay in, an acceptable rating (4 or 5 stars), and filter by the amenities you want.

You can also get an addition discount for your Norway hotel by booking on their dedicated app.

Getting around Oslo

Use the T-bane or Trams

The subway is called the t-bane. It is fast, safe and reliable. Tickets are called Ruter tickets. For day trips in zone 1 (most of the city centre) the cost is 167kr, $17. It works out much cheaper to get a 3 or 7 day ticket (287kr, $30).

Bike, Oslo is one of the easiest cities in the world to cycle. There are lots of lanes and the city is mainly flat. Cyclists like Thor Hushovd have made cycling even more popular. As a result, Norwegians generally have a very positive attitude to bicycle tourists.

Oslo City Bike (https://oslobysykkel.no) gives you unlimited rides of 45-minute duration over either 24 hours for 45kr. Buy on your phone. This is only available April to December due to icing roads during the colder months. 30 days subscription. NOK 79.

Ferries - The boats out to the islands in the Oslofjord are included in the public transportation network and can be used like any bus or subway. Grab a seat on one of the ferries and island hop between Hovedøya, Lindøya, Gressholmen, and Langøyene. Each island offers opportunities for swimming, sunbathing, barbecuing, and wild camping.

INSIDER MONEY SAVING TIP

When you pre-buy your ferry ticket make sure you get a return, they are always cheaper.
Taxi's - Don't take taxis unless you really have to. They are EXTREMELY expensive. Uber is cheaper.

Walk – it's the best way to discover Oslo, and the city is one of the safest in the world.

INSIDER MONEY SAVING TIP

REMEMBER: MiniPreis Train Tickets. Book your train tickets before you travel and save up to 80% off. Booking is simple here: https://www.vy.no/en/buy-tickets/train-tickets The more unusual time you can travel, the more you will save.

How to feel RICH in Oslo

Oslo is in a top 10 list for being home to the most million-aires. But you don't need millions in your bank to feel rich. Feeling rich feels different to every person.

"Researchers have pooled data on the relationship between money and emotions from more than 1.6 million people across 162 countries and found that **wealthier people feel more positive "self-regard emotions" such as confidence, pride and determination.**"

Here are things to see, do and taste in Oslo, that will have you overflowing with gratitude for your luxury trip to Norway.

- While money can't buy happiness, it can buy cake and isn't that sort of the same thing? Jokes aside, Åpent bakeri in Oslo have turned cakes and pastries into edible art. Visit to taste the most delicious croissant in Oslo.
- While you might not be staying in a penthouse, you can still enjoy the same views. Visit rooftop bars in Oslo, like Nodee Sky to enjoy incredible sunset views for the price of just one drink. And if you want to continue enjoying libations, head over to The Dubliner Folk Pub for a dirt-cheap happy hour, lots of reasonably priced (and delicious) cocktails and cheap delicious snacks.

Those are just some ideas for you to know that visiting Oslo on a budget doesn't have to feel like sacrifice or constriction. Now let's get into the nuts and bolts of Oslo on the super cheap.

Start with this free tour in Oslo

Kings House

Oslo is Norway's capital and largest city, with museums of national importance, incredible architecture and lively nightlife and cultural scene. The city has not always enjoyed plain sailing. In 1350, three quarter of Oslo's residents died from the Black Plague, and then in the 1600s, major fires reduced the city to ashes.

Forget exploring Oslo by wandering around aimlessly. Start with a free organised tour. Nothing compares to local advice, especially when travelling on a budget. Ask for their recommendations for the best cheap eats, the best bargains, the best markets, the best place for a particular street eat. Perhaps some of it will be repeated from this guide, but it can't hurt to ask, especially if you have specific needs or questions. At the end you should leave an appropriate tip (usually around $5), but nobody bats an eye lid if you are unable or unwilling to do so, tell them you will leave a good review and always give them a little gift from home.

This is the free tour I recommend: https://freetouroslo.com/

NORDIC FREEDOM TOURS® is a local Scandinavian brand, and offers free walking tours in Oslo. The company is run by a group of experienced guides who love to share their knowledge of this beautiful city. These free guided tours include the city's most popular attractions: Akershus Fortress, Vigeland Sculpture Park, Frognerparken, Tjuvholmen City Beach, and Huk.

A note on paying for tours
The only time paying for a tour is worth it, is when you couldn't reach the place without the tour (e.g you need a boat), or when the tour is about the same price as the attraction entry. Otherwise you can do a range of self-guided tours using for FREE.

INSIDER INSIGHT

Skip the Oslo pass: It starts at $40 a day but if you visit the attractions on the days with free admission you can save this money entirely.

Try Geocaching
This is where you hunt for hide-and-seek containers. You need a mobile device to follow the GPS clues in Norway. A typical cache is a small, waterproof container with a logbook where you can leave a message or see various trinkets left by other cache hunters. Build your own treasure

hunt by discovering geocaches in Norway.

In focus: History of Oslo

Oslo has a history that dates back more than a thousand years. In the early 19th century, the city was a small town with few inhabitants. However, during the economic boom that started in the mid-19th century, the city began to grow rapidly. As a result, people from different parts of Norway migrated to the city in search of employment. Between 1850 and 1900, the city's population increased from about 30 000 to more than two hundred thousand. The first king to live in Oslo was Haakon V, who made Oslo the de facto capital of Norway. Haakon became a powerful ruler and built the Akershus Fortress to protect the city from attacks from the Swedes. During the Viking Age, the area that became Oslo was called Viken.

Visit these Amazing Free museums in Oslo

To ensure everyone has access to culture many of Oslo's museums open their doors for free on selected days:

• Visit Oslo's National Gallery, which includes world-renowned masterpieces. It was once home to Edvard Munch's famous painting, "The Scream," but it was stolen twice! Visit on a Thursday, when entry is free.
• The Architecture Museum is inside the old headquarters of the Bank of Norway, this museum offers permanent exhibitions on the evolution of architecture over the past 200 years. Entry is free on Thursday.

• The Museum of Oslo is one for history lovers, it is a free museum located in an old farm villa which once belongs to the city's richest merchant family. It's exhibitions trace the history of the city over the past 1,000 years. FREE admission on Thursdays.

• The Museum of Contemporary Art at Bankplassen 4, features works from 1945 onwards. The exhibits here will certainly give you something to talk about. Go for free every Thursday.

• Go back in time at the Labour Museum. Hidden behind the old industrial mills along the Aker River at Sagveien 28, this museum highlights daily life for the working classes in 19th-century Oslo. FREE admission on Thursdays.

• Go Inside Oslo's City Hall, it's always free to enter and explore. The self-guided tour leads you through various rooms, each of which showcases unique art depicting Norway's historic past and political struggles for a better future. In summer they offer free guided tours.

• Visit the Bogstad Manor and Farm. Originally owned by one of Oslo's richest merchants, Adults can enjoy the pic turesque lakeside views and gardens, while kids will love meeting the animals. Touring the inside costs money, but the grounds are free to explore.

• The Armed Forces Museum located inside Akershus Fortress features Viking-era weapons, massive cannons and displays on Norway's dramatic history during the Napoleonic Wars. The museum has permanent free admission.

• The Holmenkollen Ski Jump dates back to 1892 and is a must see for fans of ski jumping. Included within the entrance fee to the ski museum (free with Oslo pass).

• The Architecture Museum, which occupies the former headquarters of the Bank of Norway, has permanent exhibitions that focus on architecture over the last 200 years. Free admission is offered on Thursdays.

• Check out the Museum of Oslo, which is located in a former farm villa of the richest merchant family in Oslo. The museum has more than 200 sculptures and is free to enter.

TOP TIP:
If you tire of all the culture go Bowling. Duckpin bowling is just $11! And if you're craving a beer afterwards the cheapest places can be found around Grønland and Tøyen in the eastern part of Oslo but they still cost around 50 NOK.

FOOD TIP:
The food vans outside the Nobel Peace Prize Museum are a great place to stop for cheap dinner before you go to a museum.

Museum's you should consider paying for:

• The Natural History Museum at the University of Oslo has a 9th century Viking ship, which is the best preserved in the world. Tickets are 150NOK ($14).
• Norway's Resistance Museum, which is a museum commemorating the history of the Norwegian occupation. Tickets are 100NOK.
• Nobel Peace Center. Admission is $7.

Visit Tjuvholmen City Beach

There are a number of beaches in Oslo that are a short walk or bus ride from the city center. These beaches are great for swimming, sunbathing, or simply relaxing.

The Tjuvholmen City Beach is situated on an island in the Oslo Fjord. This beach has a large sculpture park. You can also visit nearby attractions like the Astrup Fearnley Museum. The museum is an open air wharf gallery, with a great view of the harbor. It's free if your under 20 or 150NOK ($12), but you can also enjoy outside for free.

Pro tip: Sorenga Seawater Pool

During the summer months, locals are known to congregate at the Sorenga Seawater Pool, a modern neighborhood which stretches out into the fjords. This is one of the most popular swimming spots in the city and is a great way to cool off on a hot day.

Take a FREE guided tour of Parliament

On Saturday's you can explore Stortinget, the home of the Norwegian government on one of the two free guided daily tours. Entry is first-come, first-served, and is limited to 30 people. Go early! Book your tour here: https://www.s-tortinget.no/en/In-English/About-the-Storting/Guided-Tours-of-the-Parliament-building/

Climb the Opera House Roof

The Opera House is relatively young, having been opened in 2008. You can explore Oslo Opera House completely for free. Go up to the roof, take in the view, and explore the modern interior.

Get educated for free

In Norway education is free! Yes, even for international students. And yes, there are lots of programs taught all in English. Go get yourself a free Master's degree. The University of Oslo has a list of courses offered for free in English: https://www.uio.no/english/studies/courses/

Explore the Fjords

The Oslofjord is dotted with islands. Langøyene offers the best swimming and free camping. Take the ferry from Vippetangen Quay. Before you travel there, stock up on cheap, nutritious snacks from Grønland. An area where you will find many of the cities best cheap eats.

The tiny island of Høvedøya offers a medieval Cistercian monastery. Don't pick any plants there– many of them are descended from herbs planted by the monks centuries past, and almost all have a protected status.

On warm summer days, join swimmers and sunbathers on the rocky Huk Beach on the Bygdøy peninsula, a 25-minute bike ride west of the city. It's a public beach offers free entry to all - clothing is optional; Norwegians love to sunbathe nude.

Go to free events

Oslo's House of Literature offers weekly panel discussions on art, literature, and current events. Guest lecturers such as Haruki Murakami, John Irving, and Zadie Smith have been known to stop by. Most events are free – check their website to see what's on during your visit to Oslo: https://litteraturhuset.no/en/home/

Pack a picnic and head to the Fortress

Akershus Fortress

Oslo was a bustling port city in the Middle Ages, but the constant risks of war and fire forced the city to relocate two kilometres to a new location behind Akershus Fortress. For a perfect cheap afternoon with a view, pack a picnic and a blanket and head to Akershus Fortress. With picture-perfect views of Oslo City Hall and Aker Brygge, this is a great location to lay back, relax, and watch the sunset over the city while the ferries pass below.

This fortress is an important landmark in Oslo, and it is a great place to learn more about the city's history. The fortress was used as a prison during the 17th and 19th centuries. Today, it is a state-run facility. It has a Norwegian coat-of-arms above the door.

The fort is open every day, and there are self-guided free tours available. During the summer, you can walk through the grounds. However, it's closed during the winter.

INSIDER INSIGHT

If you're craving more great views, hike up to Grefsenåsen, a forested ridge towering over the north side of the city. From the parking lot just below the Grefsenkollen Restaurant, a short walk through the woods brings you to a rocky outcrop with magnificent views across all of Oslo.

Church Hop

Some of Norway's most fascinating buildings are its churches. Historically Norway is a Christian country, the vikings led the establishment of Christianity. Now the Evangelical Lutheran Church of Norway has the biggest denomination.

Trinity Church in the Hammersborg neighborhood shouldn't be missed. It's one of the largest churches in Oslo and most beautiful.

Step inside Oslo Cathedral, which dates from the 17th century and features a variety of artistic styles, from baroque to modern. Entry is free, as are many of the special concerts. Old Aker Church is the oldest building in Oslo. This medieval church is tucked away on a small hill in the St. Hanshaugen neighbourhood and has been in continuous use since at least the 12th century. Inside, a small museum showcases relics from the church's nearly 1,000-year history. Entry is free, but opening times can vary so check online before you visit.

Holmenkollen Chapel, which features a spectacular view of the city is beautiful. An adult Zone 1 ticket will cost 39 NOK (US$4.30)

Visit Parks and Gardens

Vigeland Park (Vigelandsanlegget)

Oslo is a very green city, one that is beautiful in spring, summer and fall. Its parks are filled with historical monuments and amazing architecture. Here are the best parks to explore in the Norwegian capital:

The **Vigeland Park** is home to over 200 granite and bronze sculptures from Gustav Vigeland that represent all stages of human life. It's located in Frogner Park. It cover 45 hectares. It features a beautiful lake in the centre. There is a walking path that you can enjoy.

These sculptures are free to visit and are also open all year round.

This park was originally created by sculptor Gustav Vigeland, who is considered to be one of the most acclaimed sculptors in the world. He was born in Mandal, Norway. Originally influenced by renaissance art, he studied in Paris, Berlin, and Florence. After studying in Europe, he returned to his hometown and began working as a sculptor. Over the years, he made several exhibitions that showcased his work.

The sculptures in the Vigeland Sculpture Park are made of cast iron, granite, and bronze. Each sculpture depicts a different stage of human life, from childhood to old age. They include statues of children, women, and men.

Once you are done at the Vigeland Sculpture Park, you can continue your visit to the nearby Vigeland Museum. The entrance to the museum is free with a Visit Oslo Pass. Although it is not the most impressive museum in the city, it is still worth the visit. At the museum, you can view the sculptures that Vigeland created in his studio.

At **Oslo's botanical gardens** you can explore over 5,500 species of plants from every corner of the world for free! St Hanshaugen Park offers amazing views across the city.

Akerselva River banks make for a lovely picnic area on a warm day.

Slottsparken, are the gardens surrounding the Royal Palace are an attraction in themselves.

Tjuvholmen Sculpture Park comes with beautiful Oslofjord views

Explore Street art

The street art scene in Oslo is one of the most vibrant in Europe. The Norwegian capital is well-known for its contemporary street art, and the Nobel Peace Center is located in an art-deco-style building that dates back to the city's former name, Christiania. The city is also known for its vibrant summer cafes.

While the city was once intolerant of graffiti and street art, new approaches to art curation have transformed the city into a vibrant and diverse urban art scene. In the past, street art in Oslo often went hand-in-hand with political protest, but nowadays it is a way of creating art and bringing beauty to the people of the city. The city has become a haven for international street artists, and the Toyen and Grunerlokka neighbourhoods are among the best places to see it. You can also spot notable pieces around the Oslo Central Station.

Visit these bargain markets

Markets are a fun and eye-opening plunge into local culture and, unless you succumb to the persistent vendors, it will cost you nothing.

Bring your appetite and visit the Oslo Food Hall at Vulkan 5. Called Mathallen in Norwegian, the food hall offers a wide range of culinary offerings from around the world. Entry is free, as is window shopping along the various food stalls, where you may be lucky enough to find some free samples on offer. Stop by the Sunday flea market at Birkelund Square in the Grünerlökka neighbourhood. You can browse the stalls of fresh farm goods, antique furniture, used books, and vintage clothing, among many other offerings.

Norway's most famous shopping street: Bogstadveien, cuts a diagonal line through the city but you won't find many bargains among the designer stores.

INSIDER MONEY SAVING TIP
Don't pay in foreign currency when buying things in places that allow you to use Euros, USD etc. They give you a really bad exchange rate and you end up losing lots of money. There are ATMs to be found almost everywhere in Oslo and you can pretty much always pay with your card.

Visit the Oldest market in Oslo: The market at Oslogate - Bispegata intersection dates back to 800 years. You'll find everything from used kitchen utensils to clothing and furniture. You can even pick up a few Norwegian delicacies! Norwegian blueberries, which are smaller than other blueberries, are particularly flavourful. You'll also find sausages, cheeses, and even handmade waffles. These traditional products are part of the national culinary canon.

Thrift shop

Thrift stores also known as charity shops or second hand shops are full of designer gems in Oslo. Bærum is one of the most expensive areas in Oslo - a little outside the city. Put it into your GPS, then put second hand shop or the American term Thrift store into Google Maps. You will be surprised by what you find in the expensive areas of Oslo.

The thrift store where I found the most bargains in Oslo is Fretex on Ullevålsveien 12.

You'll find Fretex stores in most towns and they are generally very good if you're looking for vintage & second-hand clothes.

Many tourists buy overpriced mass produced traditional Norwegian knit-wear from tourist shops. These can instead be found for a quarter or less of the price in Fretex, and are normally far more authentic and hand made.

INSIDER INSIGHT

Explore Grünerløkka. One of Oslo's coolest neighbourhood.

Its independent shops, chic cafes, and craft beer bars make for a nice afternoon to the mainstream tourist activities in Oslo.

CHEAP BOOKS: Norlis Antikvariat near the royal palace offers a huge range of paperback books for under a $1. Address: Universitetsgata 18

Go Hiking around Oslo

Østmarka

Northern Oslo consists of huge areas of pristine pine forest known as Nordmarka, and surely must be the largest, wildest backyard of any European city. More than 1200km of hiking trails make it very popular during the summer. Pick some blueberries, spot elks and go skinny-dipping.

Oslo's Royal Palace may not be as large as those in Copenhagen or Stockholm but its daily changing of the guard at 13.30 is still impressive, and free. The views from the palace hill down Karl Johan street are great.

If Norwegian nature is what you crave then hiking in Nordmarka's vast forest, just north of the city is the best you'll find. The rocky hills here have dozens of trails and cafes in small cabins, making it perfect for both short and long hikes.

Peaceful Østensjø lake on the edge of Oslo's eastern suburbs is an easy hike. Or you could take a lazy stroll or an early morning run in the mist around Sognsvann Lake. Get to Sognsvann from the subway station with the same name.

Eat For Cheap in Oslo

Kaffebrenneriet
They are part of a local chain and offer excellent service at reasonable prices. They also have great views of Aker Brygge and a large menu of coffees. They are located close to the Nobel Peace Center and Aker Brygge.

They also have alcoholic slushies and free concerts occasionally. You can check out their event schedule for what's on in Oslo. https://www.kaffebrenneriet.no/

Albertine Indisk Tandoori
'Albertine is a cosy family run restaurant with great Indian food at low prices'.The menu is stacked with a plethora of Indian cuisine, with something for everyone.

United Bakeries
A well-known bakery chain that serves up a lot of great Norwegian food.One of the coolest things about the United Bakeries is the ambiance. The place is spacious and airy, and the service is friendly. In addition, there are outdoor tables if you want to catch some rays while you're eating.

Mathallen Oslo
The food hall is home to Ma Poule, which serves duck confit sandwiches for less than 100 NOK.

Aleppo Bahebek
Located in the Vippa foodhall in Oslo's centre, Aleppo Bahebek is a social enterprise that provides the nation's best kebabs while offering a worthy cause. This isn't just a food joint, it's also a social initiative that's helping the nation's latest wave of refugees get off the ground. It's a way for the displaced to get relevant work experience while providing a much needed outlet for the locals.

Free coffee refills in Oslo

Oslo has a large community of cafes and roasteries that offer free refills. There are three places which offer free refills. Rent Mel, Godt Brød and Oslo Kaffeebar. Oslo Kaffeebar is known for its community activities, including cooking classes and home-cooking events with young refugees.

Not super cheap but loved

Try a Floating sauna

Saunas are a traditional Nordic tradition and a great way to relax. They can help you get rid of aches and pains and are great for social gatherings. In Oslo, there are several different types of saunas to choose from, including a floating sauna, which has room for up to 15 people. These saunas are open year-round, and they offer fantastic views of the fjord. KOK Oslo Sauna, Langkaia is a nice floating sauna just across the Oslo Opera House. But prices start at 1500NOK per person.

Visiting BERGEN cheaply

Bergen was once the capital of Norway and an old Hanseatic trading centre with a rich culture and dramatic scenery.

Bergen is the second largest city in Norway and the gateway to its famous fjords. Norway's second largest city is home to cute wooden buildings, a magnificent mountain setting and tons of nightlife and atmosphere. This is your gateway to the western fjords.

Aside from the fjords, Bergen is home to seven mountains. These include Mt. Sandviken, Mount Ulriken, Mount Lonahorgi, and others. You can choose to hike, or take the train to the top.

Bergen has been dubbed "the rainiest city in Europe" with an average of 250 days of rainfall a year. **Bring an umbrella.** Here are the best FREE experiences to have in Bergen:

* Bergenhus Fort. Have a picnic in the ruins of an ancient fort.
* Take a stroll around Festplassen Park 37
  * Take in the sights (and smells) of Bergen's famous fish market.
* Hike to the top of Mount Ulriken, the tallest mountain in the area. It's a moderate climb that is best done in the summer months. Another UNESCO-approved attraction is the Floyen Mountain. This mountain is the most accessible in Bergen. The mountain features several hiking trails and a troll garden.
* Take a stroll through Nordnes Park for a relaxing experience.
* If you have time, you might also consider attending one of the study days held by the Bergen-Belsen Educational Centre. These sessions allow groups to explore the history of the city in greater detail. https://bergen-belsen.stiftung-ng.de/en/educationandencounters/

And here are cheap must-see's:

* The funicular railway (Fløibanen) is one of Bergen's most famous attractions. The trip starts from the city centre, just 150 metres from Bryggen. The exciting trip up to the mountain is a magnificent experience in itself, while nature lovers will find hiking trails and pristine surroundings to enjoy at the top of Mount Fløyen. If that's still not enough for you, then the Ulriken Panoramic Tour takes you by double decker bus and cable car to 642m above the city streets, to the highest

of Bergen's famous "Seven Mountains". From the summit, you can enjoy magnificent views of Bergen and the surrounding sea, islands, fjords and mountains. And the tickets are under $4.

- The Mostraumen fjord is part of the Bergen fjord and is a narrow strait enclosed by tall mountains. It offers panoramic views of the surrounding mountains and waterfalls. Mostraumen fjord kayaking tour. There are a number of islands to explore, and you'll learn about the history of the area. https://www.viator.com/tours/Bergen/Sea-Kayaking-Rental/d4318-72238P1 just $23.
- Norwegian Glacier Museum Adults 120 NOK.

PRO TIP: GETTING TO BERGEN CHEAPLY
You can take the train from Oslo to Bergen for $33 with a Minipris ticket booked at least 8 weeks in advance. Journey time is 7 hours but you'll pass some truly mind-blowing natural sights.

Not super cheap but loved in Bergen

The Old Bergen Museum is a fun place for the whole family and its open air. With actors in costume, you'll get a chance to see how people lived in Bergen back in the 1800s. There are also a range of theatrical plays that happen daily. The museum is located in the Sandviken suburb of Bergen, a quaint area with charming wooden houses and scenic parks The museum is open year round and offers free admission for kids under 18 years of age. Admission tickets cost 120 NOK for adults. ($12)

Visit the Aurora Borealis cheaply

October to March is the best time to see the Northern Lights in Norway. The best places to see the Northern Lights in Norway are: Lyngenfjord. Bodø Lofoten Islands, Vesterålen Islands, Alta. Northern Lights in Alta, Svalbard. Due to cold weather around these times you'll have to stay in a hostel, and there are no cheap ones due to demand.

If you're visiting Sweden or thinking about visiting Sweden, the best budget Northern Lights experience is to be had at the Fjälturer hostel. By comparison it is the cheapest and best quality place to see the lights. If you go there get up at 1:30 am. This is the best time to see the show. The lights are known to be brighter and more active for up to two days after sunspot activity is at its highest. Several agencies, such as NASA and the National Oceanic and Atmospheric Administration, also monitor solar activity and issue Aurora alerts when they are expected to put on a particularly impressive show, so check their websites.

Visit TRONDHEIM cheaply

Trondheim, Norway is the third largest city in the country. It is a progressive and modern city. Located at the mouth of the Trondheim Fjord. The city was founded by Olaf Tryggvason in the early 9th century. Today, it is the oldest city in Norway. It's home to some of the country's most well-preserved medieval buildings, and boasts of a number of Michelin star restaurants.

Trondheim is compact and walkable. You can get around by foot or bike. There are several cycling paths and bike rental is cheap.

Among the attractions you may want to check out are the Old City Bridge and Nidaros Cathedral, both of which are free.

For a quick and cheap snack, you can't go wrong with a salmon sandwich at one of the many street food stalls.

Here are the best things to do in Trondheim for FREE:

- Take a walk in the forest: Trondheim Bymarkalf
  - Take the traditional tram from St. Olavs gate in the city centre and take in the great view of the city as you slowly make   your way up the city hills. TIP: Remember to take cash for   the tram (currently NOK 50 for a one-way ticket and NOK 25 for seniors over 67 and children under 16) or you can buy ina dvance from an automatic machine or the AtB office (close   to the tram stop) for a 25% discount. 42)
- Visit Nidaros Cathedral. This cathedral is the Notre Dame of the Norwegian fjords. Its tall central spire dominates the city. This Gothic-style cathedral stands over the burial site of Saint Olaf. There are several rooms hidden inside the cathedral which cost $11 to explore.
- Explore Bakklandet & be photographed on the Old Town Bridge. One of the most interesting areas in Trondheim is Bryggerekka, a ring of old wharf buildings. It is the most photogenic of all the places to visit in the city.
- Trondheim offers a variety of beaches, including the popular Lade area. If you want to do some serious fishing, head to the Orkla River. Fishing here is some of the best in Europe.
- Bymarka is another popular recreational spot. This mountain top is the highest in Trondheim, and you can find hiking trails and 200 km of cycling routes
- Rustkammeret - This museum has long been a part of the city's history. Today it is a museum that focuses on military history from the Middle Ages and its free to enter.
- If you like architecture pay a visit to Sjogata 6, a mid-19th century green timber house that was divided into four apartments. It was built by a wealthy merchant family.
- Visit Kristiansten Fortress, built to protect the city from easterly attacks. You can bring your own food and enjoy a picnic.

NOT SUPER CHEAP BUT LOVED IN TRONDHEIM

- The Archbishop's Palace is considered to be the oldest building in Scandinavia. The west wing is filled with historic displays. Inside, you can admire the Norwegian Crown Regalia. If you intend to visit the palace, jewels and catherdal buy the combination ticket. 180NOK.
- The Trondheim Science Museum, also called the Vitensenteret, is a fun and educational institution. It has a number of interactive displays. You can build games and perform experiments. There are also plenty of historical displays. 160 nok.
- Explore Norwegian music at Rockheim. A truly interactive experience. Mix your own tracks, play the guitar along with a hologram, listen to unsigned artists from across Norway, read countless old music newspapers and magazines, and a whole load more. Adults: 160,- NOK.
- Enjoy a stunning view from the Clarion Trondheim Astrum Skybar. The restaurant offers an innovative menu, and the bar offers high-quality wines from all over the world, its expensive but for one drink ($10) the view is definitely worth paying for.

Munkholmen

The small island of Munkholmen is an important tourist destination in Trondheim. There are historical sites to explore on the island, including the monastery, fortress and execution site of this former prison island. Munkholmen is accessible from Trondheim by regular boat trips. You can buy tickets on board. However, the ferry schedule may be changed, depending on rules and guidelines. Adult tickets cost 110 NOK ($9). https://www.munkholmen.no/english

PRO TIP: Drinks - Den Gode Nabo (The Good Neighbor)

Den Gode Nabo is a traditional pub in Trondheim. With wooden floors, dim lights, and a great view of the Nidelven river, and there's a good selection of local beers and pizza. There is also a courtyard, which is a lovely place to relax.

Visit Stavanger

This quaint and charming city is home to an abundance of street art and the gateway to the pulpit rock. Stavanger is a 12th century southern Norweagian city with plenty to explore. Think of it as a bigger city with a cozy historical feel.

Commercially important due to the oil business. The wooden, cobbled central area is one of the most charming places in Norway, one of Norway's medieval churches, you can visit Iron Age homes, stone age caves, and sites where the Viking kings used to meet at Ullandhaugtårnet (take bus 4 towards Madlakrossen via SUS-Madlamark).

The Stavanger museums charge expensive entrance fees so enjoy free activities in Stavanger in the great outdoors.

Here are the best free things to enjoy:

- About 15-20 minutes south of Stavanger you can find several amazing beaches and a short ferry (+ bus) ride from town you find Lysefjorden with its world famous Pulpit Rock).
- The Jæren- beaches. The vast sandy beaches of Jæren and Sola are definitely worth a visit. If the weather is nice, pack a picnic and bring your swimwear or head out for a walk or maybe even a surf! There are regular local buses leaving from Stavanger to Sola.
- Godalen and Vaulen. A 15-20 minute walk from town you find the lovely Godalen. It is a bay consisting of several little pebble beaches and green areas for summer sports, barbecuing and if the temperatures permit – swimming. Vaulen is a similar place and very popular with Stavanger people in summer. There are several buses going from town past Vaulen and it won't cost you more than 30 NOK to get there.

- In the centre of town, right by the harbour, lies the picturesque and historical Old Stavanger. It is a small area with small white painted wooden houses.

- Visit the Stavanger Cathedral, Norway's oldest stave church. It dates back to 1130 and combines materials from three previous churches. Its dark brown exterior contrasts with the green forests and blue fjord below.

- Gamle Stavanger and Ovre Holmegate are two of the most picturesque places in Stavanger. The quaint neighborhood is filled with white wooden buildings and cobblestone laneways. You can find boutique stores, independent galleries and cafes here. Ovre Holmegate is a colorful street on the other side of the harbour. As you walk down the street, you'll see rainbow-colored buildings, colorful window boxes, street art figures and a lot of people.

- Street art is a big part of Stavanger's culture. Here you can find murals, stencil art, and comic-style work. Also, be sure to check out the Sverd i fjell monument, which commemorates the Battle of Hafrsfjord.

- The Kjerag boulder hike. You will also want to try the famous Preikestolen hike. Both hikes can be done from the city center.

NOT SUPER CHEAP BUT LOVED

- Print Shop and the Oil Museum - $14 The Petroleum Museum, for example, is a fascinating museum that explores the history of oil and gas in Norway.

- Viking House, a tourist centre that features a life-like VR film. It depicts the story of King Harald Fairhair. Entry is $20.

- One of the most spectacular fjords in the world, Lyesfjord is the heart of the Stavanger region. RIB safaris are a popular activity on the fjord. You can get close to the rock faces and take pictures of the water. Expect to pay $120 each.

Visit the Pulpit Rock on the cheap

Instead of taking a guided tourist route there, take the local ferry from Stavanger to Tau for 46 NOK for an adult. The bus from Tau to the Pulpit Rock base is 160 for a return ticket. Bring your own food and drinks as the prices on the ferry and the kiosk at the Pulpit Rock base are VERY high.

Pulpit Rock is one of the most beautiful places in the country. The best time to visit is early in the morning. You can avoid the crowds and get some good pictures. Spend the entire morning or afternoon soaking up the scenery.

Go Hiking in the Lofoten islands

Bodø is the gateway to the magnificent Lofoten islands and Saltstraumen, the worlds strongest maelstrom. King Øystein built a church and lodgings for fishermen here in 1120. The best thing to experience in Lofoten for free are the hikes. Here are the best:

Reinebringen Hiking to the top of Reinebringen

It gives a bird's eye view of the archipelago of the tiny Lofoten islands and the narrow E10 road that connects them like a string of pearls. From the summit ridge looking down gives is a great vantage point to see the fjords of Reine. It's a short but steep hike to get to the top but the rewarding panorama at the top more than makeup for all the hard work. Duration: 2-3 hours Max elevation: 448 mts.

Bunes beach

Bunes beach is one of the ideal spots to see the midnight sun caress the horizon and come back up during summers. The long streaks of golden on the water left us spellbound. The trailhead can be reached by taking a ferry from Reine towards Vindstad. This side of the Moskenesoya island is really remote except for a few houses at the ferry quay. This an easy walk with the trail gradually ascending up to a pass and then down to the beach. A great option is to skip the ferry and instead kayak from Reine and end it with this hike like we did. Duration: 1-2 hours Hiking the dunes beach in Lofoten

Horseid beach hiking horse beach in the lofoten island

The dune filled Horseid beach faces the Norwegian sea and requires hiking up a short mountain pass to the other side. The swaying tall grass on one end and the thrashing sea waves on the other and tall mountains make up for a great frame, characteristic of the Lofoten islands. There is ample flat ground to pitch a tent and experience the magical spell of the midnight sun in the summers. The easiest access to the trailhead is through a ferry from Reine. We felt most desolate on this beach and appeased our tired legs walking barefoot on the soft sand. Duration: 2-3 hours

Djevelporten (Devil's gate), is the infamous rock wedged between Frosken and Fløya. Start the hike at Svolvær.

Justandinten is an easy and very well-worn trail through a scenic mountain landscape to the summit of Justadtinden. Around the Lofoten islands look out for Orca's and cheeky seals. Orca's are most common around the vesterålen coast, north of Bødo.

Visit Ålesund

This colourful town is a myriad of turrets, spires and beautiful ornamentation full of art nouveau buildings and breathtaking Fjords and a lot of cheap and free activities. It is the perfect base from which to explore the Norwegian fjords and mountains.

The city's Art Nouveau heart features ornate balconies and decorative archways. The buildings were built during the romantic period and they glow when the sun passes through the thick cloud cover.

Alesund is also home to several museums. The Sykkylven Furniture Museum pays tribute to the rich history of furniture making in the region. Another museum in the area is the Ivar Aasen Center. It is located on the famous poet's farm. The Sykkylven Nature Museum is also worth a visit, especially if you are interested in native animals. The museum features a large collection of native animals, and is popular with you. Tickets are 70 NOK ($6).

In focus: Ålesund's-Art Nouveau centre

The city is known for its architectural charm, which was the result of a devastating fire in 1904. A large number of timber houses and buildings were damaged in the blaze, leaving 10,000 people homeless. Officials in Alesund worked with top master builders and architects to rebuild the town and thus the art nouveau centre was born.

Alesund's buildings are full of asymmetrical spires, elegant organic lines, and colourful decorations. These buildings are part of a European network of Art Nouveau cities.

The first stop on the Art Nouveau city center tour is by-parken, a park that features copper beech trees, a monkey puzzle tree, and a statue of Rollo. You'll also see a statue of the Herring Wife, a sculpture that is a tribute to women who worked at the salting herring industry. Following the park, you'll walk through the streets of Alesund.

Stop at Apotekergata 16, one of the best examples of Alesund's Art Nouveau architecture, is a former chemist's shop. It now houses the Art Nouveau Center, which is a must-see.

There are plenty of Art Nouveau museums in and around Alesund. One of the most interesting is the Jugendstilsenteret (110 NOK), which is both a museum and the national center of Art Nouveau.

PRO TIP: Pick up a free guide from a tourist office.

Here are the best free things to see in Alesund:

- Fjellstua viewpoint. This is a view of the town, the sea and the Sunnmore Alps. And it is also a great photo opportunity. The best way to reach this viewpoint is by car or public transportation. For this reason, you may want to hire a private guide to make the most of your limited time on the quay.
- Hike to Sunnmore Alps to get an incredible viewpoint over the town.
- To experience the best of Ålesund kayak to Hessa island and hike to Sukkertoppen mountain
- If you want to know what life is like in a small fishing village in Norway Take bus 662 to the islands of Giske and Godoy: These islands are connected to Alesund via a long, undersea tunnel.
- Another free thing to do in Alesund is to visit the Museum of Sunnmore. Here, you can learn about the city's history and enjoy a large collection of old boats. There are also free guided tours at the Sunnmore Museum. During this free tour, you can explore the historical buildings and exhibits. These buildings are located within a beautiful, open-air landscape. It is also home to a replica of the Viking ships.

Here are the best cheap things to see:

- If you're more into culture visit Ålesund Church. It costs $5 to go inside but the stain glass windows make it worth paying.
- Visit the Alesund Aquarium/ Alesund Atlantic Sea Park (and a hike along the trails nearby): NOK 90 .

NOT SUPER CHEAP BUT LOVED

Geiranger Fjord

The fjord is a UNESCO World Heritage Site, and a popular destination for sightseeing. Taking a trip by RIB boat is a great way to see the beautiful scenery. RIB Geiranger - Price from NOK 295 or you can cheaply kayak around the fjord or simply enjoy it from land.

Not Super Cheap but maybe worth it in Norway

Experience The World's Northernmost Igloo Hotel

'Feel the magic. at Sorrisniva igloo hotel. Witness the detailed works of art. And enter a frozen world of possibilities. At Sorrisniva, they build a brand new Igloo Hotel during early winter. You can book a guided tour, or even stay overnight in the Arctic icon of snow and ice. The prices for glass igloo stay start from $243 per night'. https://www.sorrisniva.no/

FOOD AND DRINK HACKS for Norway

Do NOT buy bottled water. Norwegian tap water tastes great and most of the bottled water is from the same source as tap water. Save money and the environment by filling your empty bottle with water from the tap and ask for tap water at restaurants.

Buy supermarket own brand It tastes the same as brands and will save you a fortune on costly imported brands.

A beer in Norway is $15, pre-drink before you go out. The locals call the practice forspill.

Eat Mexican street food in Oslo. Cielito is a Mexican restaurant at Dronningens Gate 26. Mexican food comes in the cheapest eats across Oslo.

Stock up on magic bags in Oslo before you venture further afield. Or visit supermarkets in Lofoten and the other areas around 4pm when they knock 50% off the fresh produce prices.

Best bang for your buck all-you-can-eat

All you can eat buffets are a great way to stock on on nutritious food while travelling and there are plenty in Norway. Jaipur Restaurant in Oslo offers traditional Indian all you can eat for 99kr at lunch, just $11!

Tipping

You don't have to tip. Tipping in Norway is not obligatory and in most situations not expected due to high salaries.

Must-try Norwegian Foods

Norwegian food is protein heavy, made for long-hard winters. The best dishes to try in Norway are:

A. Kjøttkaker. This simple dish is common throughout the country and many families eat it weekly.
B. Lefse. Norwegians love this sweetened variety of the traditional soft flatbread with a cup of coffee.
C. Kumla – Tender Potato Dumplings.
D. Lutefisk – Gelatinous Fish Dish.
E. Whale Steak – Famous Junk-Food Dish from Whale Meat.
F. Pickled Herring – Ancient Viking-style Pickle.
G. Krumkake – similar to a Sicilian cannoli, a biscuit shell stuffed with cream.
H. Fårikål – National Dish of Norway. A mutton casserole.
I. Mackol og masegg. This is a traditional Northern Norwegian seasonal dish. This is a stew that is made of a mix-

ture of meats and potatoes. It is usually served on flat-bread with dairy butter. The dish is often served with beer.

J. Farepolse, which is made of dried meat from lamb. It is served as a topping for bread or as a side.

Cheap Eats

Fill your stomach without emptying your wallet by trying these local places with mains under $10.

(Download the offline map on google maps, (instructions 1. go to app 2. select offline apps in the left sidebar 3. go to the area you want to download 4. click download). Then simply type the restaurant names in to navigate, star them so you can see where the cheap eats are when you're out and about to avoid wasting your money at hyped tourist joints)

There are plenty of good options for budget-conscious travellers in Oslo. Outside Oslo it gets EXPENSIVE, so, unfortunately, we cannot recommend any restaurants in other cities. Outside Oslo its best to buy Supermarket own brand and cook on your tent stove or at your hostel/ Airbnb.

Marie Peyre. Punjab Tandoori
This popular Indian restaurant in Grønland was one of the first to open in Oslo back in 1990, and it is still going strong. Here you will find authentic Punjab food at bargain prices, with mains starting at 80kr. Their naan bread is legendary. Queues are not unusual, so just don't expect to linger once you have finished your meal.

Freddy Fuego
An informal burrito bar with long tables to eat out with friends before a night out on the town, rather than a romantic dinner with a date. But the food here packs a punch. Each burrito is freshly made to order with your choice of meat, salsa and extras. .

Krishna's Cuisine
Located in the Colosseum Centre in Majorstua, this long standing restaurant serves good vegetarian food, with veg-

an alternatives too. Soup of the day, served with rice or pappadum, costs 90kr. Big salad 100kr. Lunch plate 120kr. The dish of the day costs 150kr, and comes with a free refill, should you still be hungry. Closing time is 8 pm.

Hai Café

Classics such as Vietnamese spring rolls, pho and bánh mì make up the bulk of the menu here, and that's really what most people order. With its relaxed vibe, Hai Café is great for a late lunch or early dinner. Prices are cheap. The best of several Vietnamese restaurants in the Torggata area.

Hell's Kitchen

Cool American-style booths, a good selection of beers, and great thin pizzas.

Munchies

In the mood for a burger? Check out Munchies. The menu is short and sweet, with six burgers to choose from, four of them under 100kr. A bargain in Oslo. You can customize your order with sauces like mango curry, jalapeño, BBQ or aioli. Open late.

Ma Poule

Located inside Mathallen (literally, 'the food hall') in Vulkan, Ma Poule is one of the several joints offering a small selection of dishes at reasonable prices, like their best-selling duck confit sandwich for under 100kr. The chicken sandwich at Stangeriet next door is also good.

Meatballs

Opened in June 2016, this restaurant in Hausmanns gate is Oslo's first meatball-joint. Beef, pork, chicken, veggie, all the 'meatballs' here are handmade on the premises and served with tasty sauces and sides. The meat comes from the best local suppliers, with traceable origin. Three-balls combo for 97kr.

Rice Bowl Thai Café

Address: Kirkegata 20
Amazing cheap Thai with bamboo & wall hangings, serving traditional noodle & curry dishes.

Tuk Tuk Thai

Address: Møllergata 8
Must try Thai restaurant in Oslo Sentrum.

Green Taste take-away
Address: Oslo gate 39
A well kept secret kept on the east side of the city serving incredible Vietnamese.

TUNCO
Asian food for low-prices.

Gazakjøkken
Popular Falafel place.

Palmyra Cafe
Address: Norbygata 15A
Sri Lankan food in a cozy setting with great prices.

Syverkiosken
Cheap Hot Dog Stand
Address: Maridalsveien 45B

Sofies mat og vinhus
Address: Sofies gate 15
Cheap fish and generous portions.

Carmel grill
Address: Dronningens Gate 27
Huge delicious kebabs.

Krishnas Cuisine
Address: Sørkedalsveien 10 · In Colosseum Center
Simple but delicious vegetarian /vegan food.

King Falafel
Address: Brugata 3A · In Youngstorget

Sea Sushi
Cheap but delicious Sushi.
Address: Toftes Gate 20

East Kitchen
Address: Markveien 50A
Very good sushi and a cute shop

Dalat Cafe
Vietnamese with the best pork pho you'll ever try.
Address: Torggata 27

Avoid these tourist traps or scams

Scams and trickery are the scourge of a traveler's budget and unfortunately Scams abound near the attractions. If someone approaches you and you fear their intentions just say 'sorry, no english.' and walk on.

Common tourist scams
1. Avoid eating in restaurants near attractions, go down a sidestreet and prices will drop significantly in Oslo.
2. Distraction thief is on the rise in Oslo. Don't keep things in your back pockets or in easily unzipped bags.
3. If you are approached in the street to sign a petition to support a charity, politely refuse to do so. Often, if you do sign you will be pressured to give a donation. Should it look like you are going to refuse to pay, an accomplice will usually try to pick your pockets while you are distracted and arguing with the other scammer.
Outside Oslo scams are few and far between.

Religion

Religion in Norway is strongly Lutheran Christianity, 69.9% % of the nation identify as Evangelical Lutheran Church of Norway and the church plays a strong role in family life here.

Basic Phrases

Tusen takk which means thanks very much will be appreciated in in shops and restaurants.

English ▾   ⇄   Norwegian ▾

English	Norwegian
Hi	Hei
Please	Vær så snill
Bye	Ha det
Thank you	Takk skal du ha
How Much is it?	Hvor mye er det?
Where is the bus?	Hvor er bussen?
Where is the train?	Hvor er toget?

Getting Out

Train
Booking ahead can save you up to 80% of the cost of the ticket with the mini preis tickets. Book here:

Bus
Flixbus, Polski bus and regiojet are the cheapest buses for onward cities from Norway. Booking ahead can save you up to 98% of the cost of the ticket.

Plane
At the time of writing Wizz Air (Wizz Air has a base at Norway airport) are offering flights to 25 cities for less than $20. Take advantage of discounts and specials. Sign up for e-newsletters from local carriers including Wizz Air to learn about special fares. Be careful with cheap airlines, most will allow hand-luggage only, and some charge for anythi

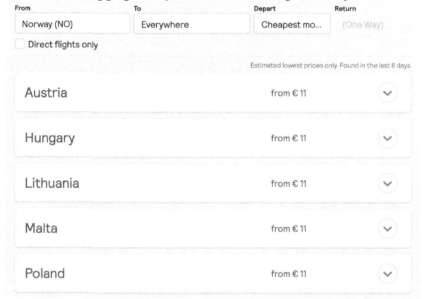

ng that is not a backpack. Check their websites before

booking if you need to take luggage.

Airport Lounges

You don't need to be flying business or first class to enjoy an airport lounge. Here are three methods you can use to access lounges at Norway airport:

- Get or use a credit card that gives free lounge access. NerdWallet has a good write-up about cards that offer free lounge access. www.nerdwallet.com/best/credit-cards/airport-lounge-access

- Buy onetime access. They start at $23 and often include free showers and free drinks and food.

- Find free access with the LoungeBuddy app. You pay an annual fee of $25 to use the app.

Interesting Facts About Norway

Norway's first inhabitants lived primarily by hunting and fishing. But after about 3,000 BC, farming took hold. Stone tools were the norm, but the people later began to use bronze tools. Around two thousand years ago, the Norwegians started writing with runes. Their ancestors were the Vikings, famous for raiding France, England, Scotland, Ireland, and Spain.

The Law of Jante is an important part of Norwegian culture

Norwegian culture has a long history and is a rich and varied one. Norwegians generally adhere to the Law of Jante, which promotes collective social well-being and gender equality. It also helps build a common ground between different groups. For instance, Norwegians don't refer to other people with honorific titles, and they prefer to address people by their first names only.

Norwegians are also very humble. It is difficult for them to brag, and they often criticize people for looking big-headed. People like Sarkozy and Berlusconi could never hold state offices in Norway, because the people in Norway would never accept it.

The Sami are a distinct culture

The Sami are a culturally distinct group of people living in northern Scandinavia. They have a history that spans centuries.

The Sami culture has its own distinct language and cultural expression. The language has equal status with Norwegian, meaning that those living in Sami-speaking areas are entitled to services in Sami. Several road signs are bilingual, and the national broadcaster produces content in the language. In addition, the NRK Sapmi radio station is broadcast nationwide via DAB, and also online.

Although Sami organizations were established for centuries, national Sami organizations did not form until the Second World War. At that time, people involved in Sami causes were viewed as extremists and dreamers. However, after the war, they began to flourish and make an impact on society.

The Sami population is estimated at about 75,000 people. However, this figure is subject to debate because official censuses have not provided reliable counts. Despite their distinct culture, the Sami are now assimilated by the Norwegian culture. They speak a language that belongs to the Finno-Ugric branch of the Uralic family and is closely related to Baltic Sea-Finnish languages.

Norway Monarchy

Norway has a constitutional monarchy, and the king exercises limited power. He appoints a prime minister, who acts as head of government. A unicameral legislature, the Storting, has 165 seats. In 2001, the Parliament was divided between eight parties. Elections are held every four years. The government does not always win these elections, and the prime minister may change as needed to stay in power.

Bouvet Island is the most remote island in the world

Bouvet Island is located in the North Atlantic Ocean. The island was first discovered in 1739 by Jean Baptiste Charles Bouvet de Lozier, but the island was lost due to wrong coordinates. The Norwegians first came ashore in 1927, and in 1928, a Norvegia expedition claimed it. The island was then handed to Norway, and Norway was able to claim it after protesting that Britain had planted a Union flag on the island in 1825.

Bouvet Island is the most remote island on earth. It is a volcanic island surrounded by glaciers and is located 2,200 kilometers south of South Africa. It was claimed by the British in 1825, but no expeditions visited the island until the late 19th century. In 1929, the UK waived its claim on the island. By then, Norway had occupied the island and designated it as a nature reserve. Bouvet Island is surrounded by high glacial cliffs, and access to it requires a helicopter landing on a patch of ice. There are no roads to the island and only offshore anchorages, making it impossible to reach it by car. The island has no electricity, plumbing, or year-round human residents.

Bouvet Island is home to 422 ringed penguins and over six thousand fur seals. The island is also home to a small unmanned weather station.

Personal Cost Breakdown

	How	Cost normally	Actual Cost
How I got from the airport to the city	train	$65 Taxi	$11
Where I stayed	Wild camped. Hostel or cheaper Airbnb outside the city limits.	$250 hotel average	$15 a night
Tastiest street foods I ate and cost	salmon, flat breads, verdens beste (a cream cake with straweberries)		$5 average meal
How I got around	Bike Minipreis tickets	Oslo is such a lovely city to cycle.	$100
What I saw and paid	Palaces, castles, museums, gardens and so much grandeur, hikes, Fjords, waterfalls	$200	$0 (visit during the free times)
My on ward flight	London	Book ahead to save up to $100 on flights/ buses	$13
My Total costs			US$250

Print or screenshot for easy reference

	How	Cost
Get from the airport	book your train ticket from the airport to the city	$11
Stay	wild camp	$60 - sending camping equipment fee.
Food	Average meal cost: $6 – $12 - see cheap eats section.	$8 per meal
Get around	T-bane, trams and cycle	$30 for all rides for 7 days or bike for free.
See	Museums and galleries on their free days, hikes, Fjords and breath-taking nature	$0
Best discounts	MiniPreis tickets	0
Get out	Onward flight to London	$13
Total		$250

PRACTICAL THINGS TO REMEMBER TO SAVE MONEY

If you plan to wild camp ask friends to lend you equipment or source from thrift stores to save mon ey. Before you book your flight, check the airlines baggage prices. Sometimes paying more for the flight can save you money on checking baggage. Alternatively you could send your camping gear ahead with send-mybag.com Make sure you pack raingear. There is no bad weather, just bad clothing is a maxim the Norwegians live by.

Bring lemongrass oil in summer and mix it with a moisturiser for a cheap, natural and effective mos quito repellent. Rub it everywhere, the areas you don't cover will be bitten. This is the same method the Inca's used.

Look at sendmybag.com to see if it's cheaper to send your pack to a hostel or airbnb rather than flying with it.

Download a local weather app (Yr by NRK is locally used) as nordic weather is highly unpredictable.

Download google maps for for use offline in Oslo and any other area you plan to visit. You can find good free maps from the tourist offices.

Download the language packet for Norwegian, many people over the age of 50 don't speak English.

Know the names of foods to try and star some restaurants on Google maps to try them in.

Use Uber if you need to take a taxi. Local taxi's

charge three times the price of an Uber.

Book your minipris tickets for train travel before you travel: this can save you 80%

Make a list of the museums you want to visit in Oslo and mark their free days in your calendar.

Avoid over-scheduling in Oslo. You don't want to pack so much into your trip you wind up feeling like you're working on the conveyor belt called best sights of Oslo instead of fully saturating your senses in the incredible sights, sounds, smells of Oslo.

RECAP: How to Enjoy a $5,000 trip to Norway for $250

Find a cheap flight
Using the strategy we outlined you can snag a ticket to Norway from the states from $300 return. From the EU budget carrier Ryanair is flying to Norway from $5! Potential saving $1,000.

Take advantage of allemannsretten (meaning "freedom to roam")
In the high season, you can be looking at $150 a night for an Airbnb or hostel. Plan to wild camp for free and save yourself thousands on a longer trip. As long as you come prepared and take every available weight saving measure camping is easy in Norway. Check https://mapcarta.com/N4408689303 for up to date wild camping coordinates. Potential saving $4000.

Book Mini Preis tickets
Book your train tickets 8 weeks before you travel to save 80% of the cost. Potential saving $300.

Check out repositioning cruises
You can save 70% on a cruise of Norway! Potential savings: $3,000

Use too good to go

Save an absolute fortune on foods by picking up magic bags from over 5,000 restaurants, bakeries, ice cream parlous and supermarkets located all over Norway. And remember never buy a bag without rating and never with ratings under 4.2 stars. It's also worth noting a lot of hotels offer great breakfast buffer magic bags but some are a total waste of time in Norway. Check the reviews before purchasing. Potential saving: $500

Rent a car from a Norwegian
Use GetAround to rent a car from a person in Norway and save an fortune on car rental. potential saving: $1,500.

Five star hotels in Oslo
Last minute 5 star hotels deals. Check on the same day of your stay for cheap five star hotel deals. Go to enter Oslo tonight, only one night and filtears. This can be very effective during the low season on weekends when hotels empty of their business travellers. Potential saving $800.

Go to museums/ attractions on their free days
The average traveller spends $180 on museums in Oslo, but there's no need if you indulge in Viking relics and art on the days the museums have free entry. Potential saving $180.

Do all the free stuff first
The natural environment in Norway is an endless bounty of interesting and inspiring things to experience. Start free and be mindful of what you want to pay for. Potential savings: $500.

Supermarket deals
Nearly every supermarket in Norway offers 50% discounts after 4pm. Potential saving $200.

Drink outdoors with friends

Norway is super green and the best way to experience the city is to buy a couple of beers from a supermarket and enjoy them somewhere green. **A beer costs around $15 in a bar in Norway**. Potential savings on drinks $200.

Book Ahead

Book six weeks ahead for the lowest prices on outward buses and flights. Potential savings: $100

Money Mistakes in Norway

Cost	Impact	Solution	Note
Using your home currency	Some credit card rates charge for every transaction in another currency. Check carefully before you use it	Use a prepaid currency card like Wise Multi-Currency Debit Card.	
Not camping	Accommodation in Norway averages at $250 a night... camping is FREE.	Camp or stay in Hytte.	Send your camp gear to a hostel with sendmybag.com for much less than airlines charge.
Buying bottled water	At $3 a bottle, this is a cost that can mount up quickly	Refill from the tap.	
Eating like a tourist	Eating at tourist traps can triple your bill. Choose wisely	Star cheap eats on google maps so you're never far from one	
Forgetting essenitals	Because Norway is expensive forgetting sunscreen and other essentials can cost you.	Pack your essentials to last the duration of your trip.	
Not agreeing a price of everything in advance	Taxi's and other unpriced services allow people to con you..	Agree the price beforehand to avoid unwanted bills	
Not getting your VAT refund	20% of all sales purchases		It is not Norwegian Customs who reimburses VAT. You must inquire with the store in which you bought the goods on how you may have Norwegian VAT reimbursed.

The secret to saving HUGE amounts of money when travelling to Norway is...

Your mindset. Money is an emotional topic, if you associate words like cheapskate, Miser (and its £9.50 to go into Charles Dickens Norway house, oh the Irony) with being thrifty when traveling you are likely to say 'F-it' and spend your money needlessly because you associate pain with saving money. You pay now for an immediate reward. Our brains are prehistoric; they focus on surviving day to day. Travel companies and hotels know this and put trillions into making you believe you will be happier when you spend on their products or services. Our poor brains are up against outdated programming and an onslaught of advertisements bombarding us with the message: spending money on travel equals PLEASURE. To correct this carefully lodged propaganda in your frontal cortex, you need to imagine your future self.

Saving money does not make you a cheapskate. It makes you smart. How do people get rich? They invest their money. They don't go out and earn it; they let their money earn more money. So every time you want to spend money, imagine this: while you travel, your money is working for you, not you for money. While you sleep, the money, you've invested is going up and up. That's a pleasure a pricey entrance fee can't give you. Thinking about putting your money to work for you tricks your brain into believing you are not withholding pleasure from yourself, you are saving your money to invest so you can go to even more amazing places. You are thus turning thrifty travel into a pleasure fueled sport.

When you've got money invested - If you want to splash your cash on a first-class airplane seat - you can. I can't tell you how to invest your money, only that you should. Saving $20 on taxis doesn't seem like much, but over time you could save upwards of $15,000 a year, which is a deposit for a house which you can rent on Airbnb to finance more travel. Your brain making money looks like your brain on cocaine, so tell yourself saving money is making money.

Scientists have proved that imagining your future self is the easiest way to associate pleasure with saving money. You can download FaceApp — which will give you a picture of what you will look like older and grayer, or you can take a deep breath just before spending money and ask yourself if you will regret the purchase later.

The easiest ways to waste money traveling are:

Getting a taxi. The solution to this is to always download the google map before you go. Many taxi drivers will drive you around for 15 minutes when the place you were trying to get to is a 5-minute walk... remember while not getting an overpriced taxi to tell yourself, 'I am saving money to free myself for more travel.'
Spending money on overpriced food when hungry. The solution: carry snacks. A banana and an apple will cost you, in most places, less than a dollar.

Spending on entrance fees to top-rated attractions. If you really want to do it, spend the money happily. If you're conflicted, sleep on it. I don't regret spending $200 on a sky dive over the Great Barrier Reef; I regret going to the top of the shard on a cloudy day in London for $60. Only you can know, but make sure it's your decision and not the marketing directors at said top-rated attraction.

Telling yourself 'you only have the chance to see/eat/experience it now'. While this might be true, make sure YOU WANT to spend the money. Money spent is money you can't invest, and often you can have the same experience for much less.

You can experience luxurious travel on a small budget, which will trick your brain into thinking you're already a high-roller, which will mean you'll be more likely to act like one and invest your money. Stay in five-star hotels for $5 by booking on the day of your stay on booking.com to enjoy last-minute deals. You can go to fancy restaurants using daily deal sites. Ask your airline about last-minute upgrades to first-class or business. I paid $100 extra on a $179 ticket to Cuba from Germany to be bumped to Business Class. When you ask, it will surprise you what you can get both at hotels and airlines.

Travel, as the saying goes, is the only thing you spend money on that makes you richer. You can easily waste money, making it difficult to enjoy that metaphysical wealth. The biggest money saving secret is to turn bargain hunting into a pleasurable activity, not an annoyance. Budgeting consciously can be fun, don't feel disappointed because you don't spend the $60 to go into an attraction. Feel good because soon that $60 will soon earn money for you. Meaning, you'll have the time and money to enjoy more metaphysical wealth while your bank balance increases.

So there it is. You can save a small fortune by being strategic with your trip planning. We've arranged everything in the guide to offer the best bang for your buck. Which means we took the view that if it's not an excellent investment for your money, we wouldn't include it. Why would a guide called 'Super Cheap' include lots of overpriced attractions? That said, if you think we've missed something or have unanswered questions, ping me an email: philgtang@gmail.com I'm on central Europe time and usually reply within 8 hours of getting your mail. We like to think of our guide books as evolving organisms helping our readers travel better cheaper. We use reader questions via email to update this book year round so you'll be helping other readers and yourself.

Don't put your dreams off!

Time is a currency you never get back and travel is its greatest return on investment. Plus, now you know you can visit Norway for a fraction of the price most would have you believe.

Thank you for reading

Dear **Lovely Reader**,

If you have found this book useful, please consider writing a quick review on Amazon.

One person from every 1000 readers leaves a review on Amazon. It would mean more than you could ever know if you were one of our 1 in 1000 people to take the time to write a brief review.

Thank you so much for reading again and for spending your time and investing your trips future in Super Cheap Insider Guides.

One last note, please don't listen to anyone who says 'Oh no, you can't visit Norway on a budget'. Unlike you, they didn't have this book. You can do ANYWHERE on a budget with the right insider advice and planning. Sure, learning to travel to Norway on a budget that doesn't compromise on anything or drastically compromise on safety or comfort levels is a skill, but this guide has done the detective work for you. Now it is time for you to put the advice into action.

Phil and the Super Cheap Insider Guides Team

P.S If you need any more super cheap tips we'd love to hear from you e-mail me at philgtang@gmail.com, we have a lot of contacts in every region, so if there's a specific bargain you're hunting we can help you find it.

DISCOVER YOUR NEXT VACATION

☑ **LUXURY ON A BUDGET APPROACH**

☑ **CHOOSE FROM 107 DESTINATIONS**

☑ **EACH BOOK PACKED WITH REAL-TIME LOCAL TIPS**

All are available in Paperback and e-book on Amazon:
https://www.amazon.com/dp/B09C2DHQG5

Bonus Travel Hacks

I've included these bonus travel hacks to help you plan and enjoy your trip to Norway cheaply, joyfully, and smoothly.

Common pitfalls when it comes to allocating money to <u>your desires</u> while traveling

Know the exchange rate

If you're traveling from the states to Indonesia, your one dollar is worth 10,800 rupiah. When your is wallet stuffed with high-denomination bills, you'll less likely to remember the exchange rate. Remember, it's not monopoly money, it's your money and you should consciously choose to spend it on things you desire. At the time of writing, 1 dollar is 11.17kr in Norway.

Beware of Malleable mental accounting

Let's say you budgeted spending only $30 per day in Norway but then you say well if I was at home I'd be spending $30 on food as an everyday purchase so you add another $30 to your budget. Don't fall into that trap as the likelihood is you still have expenses at home even if its just the cost of keeping your freezer going.

Beware of impulse purchases in Norway

Restaurants that you haven't researched and just idle into can sometimes turn out to be great, but more often, they turn out to suck, especially if they are near tourist attractions. Make yourself a travel itinerary including where you'll eat breakfast and lunch. Dinner is always more expensive, so the meal best to enjoy at home or as a takeaway. This book is full of incredible cheap eats. All you have to do is plan to go to them.

Social media and FOMO (Fear of Missing Out)

'The pull of seeing acquaintances spend money on travel can often be a more powerful motivator to spend more while traveling than seeing an advertisement.' Beware of what you allow to influence you and go back to the question, what's the best money I can spend today?

Now-or-never sales strategies

One reason tourists are targeted by salespeople is the success of the now-or-never strategy. If you don't spend the money now… your never get the opportunity again. Rarely is this true.

Instead of spending your money on something you might not actually desire, take five minutes. Ask yourself, do I really want this? And return to the answer in five minutes. Your body will either say an absolute yes with a warm, excited feeling or a no with a weak, obscure feeling.

Unexpected costs

"Holding on to anger is like grasping a hot coal with the intent of throwing it at someone else; you only hurt yourself." The Buddha.

One downside to traveling is unexpected costs. When these spring up from airlines, accommodation providers, tours and on and on, they feel like a punch in the gut. During the pandemic my earnings fell to 20% of what they are normally. No one was traveling, no one was buying travel guides. My accountant out of nowhere significantly raised his fee for the year despite the fact there was a lot less money to count. I was so angry I consulted a lawyer who told me you will spend more taking him to court than you will paying his bill. I had to get myself into a good feeling place before I paid his bill, so I googled how to feel good paying someone who has scammed you.

The answer: Write down that you will receive 10 times the amount you are paying from an unexpected source. I did that. Four months later, the accountant wrote to me. He had applied for a COVID subsidy for me and I would receive… you guessed it almost exactly 10 times his fee.

Make of that what you want. I don't wish to get embroiled in a conversation about what many term 'woo-woo', but the result of my writing that I would receive 10 times the amount made me feel much, much better when paying him. And ultimately, that was a gift in itself. So next time some airline or train operator or hotel/ Airbnb sticks you with an unexpected fee, immediately write that you will receive 10 times the amount you are paying from an unexpected source. Rise your vibe and skip the added price of feeling angry.

Hack your allocations for your Norway Trip

"The best trick for saving is to eliminate the decision to save." Perry Wright of Duke University.

Put the money you plan to spend in Norway on a pre-paid card in the local currency. This cuts out two problems - not knowing how much you've spent and totally avoiding expensive currency conversion fees.

You could even create separate spaces. This much for transportation, this for tours/entertainment, accommodation and food. We are reluctant to spend money that is pre-assigned to categories or uses.

Write that you want to enjoy a $3,000 trip for $500 to your Norway trip. Countless research shows when you put goals in writing, you have a higher chance of following through.

Spend all the money you want to on buying experiences in Norway

"Experiences are like good relatives that stay for a while and then leave. Objects are like relatives who move in and stay past their welcome." Daniel Gilbert, psychologist from Harvard University.

Economic and psychological research shows we are happier buying brief experiences on vacation rather than buying stuff to wear so give yourself freedom to spend on experiences knowing that the value you get back is many many times over.

Make saving money a game

There's one day a year where all the thrift shops where me and my family live sell everything there for a $1. My wife and I hold a contest where we take $5 and buy an entire outfit for each other. Whoever's outfit is liked more wins. We also look online to see whose outfit would have cost more to buy new. This year, my wife even snagged me an Armani coat for $1. I liked the coat when she showed it to me, but when I found out it was $500 new; I liked it and wore it a lot more.

Quadruple your money

Every-time you want to spend money, imagine it quadrupled. So the $10 you want to spend is actually $40. Now imagine that what you want to buy is four times the price. Do you still want it? If yes, go enjoy. If not, you've just saved yourself money, know you can choose to invest it in a way that quadruples or allocate it to something you really want to give you a greater return.

Understand what having unlimited amounts of money to spend in Norway actually looks like

Let's look at what it would be like to have unlimited amounts of money to spend on your trip to Norway.

Isolation

You take a private jet to your private Norway hotel. There you are lavished with the best food, drink, and entertainment. Spending vast amounts of money on vacation equals being isolated.

If you're on your honeymoon and you want to be alone with your Amore, this is wonderful, but it can be equally wonderful to make new friends. Know this a study 'carried out by Brigham Young University, Utah found that while obesity increased risk of death by 30%, loneliness increased it by half.'

Comfort

Money can buy you late check outs of five-star hotels and priority boarding on airlines, all of which add up to comfort. But as this book has shown you, saving money in Norway doesn't minimize comfort, that's just a lie travel agencies littered with glossy brochures want you to believe.

You can do late-check outs for free with the right credit cards and priority boarding can be purchased with a lot of airlines from $4. If you want to go big with first-class or business, flights offset your own travel costs by renting your own home or you can upgrade at the airport often for a fraction of what you would have paid booking a business flight online.

MORE TIPS TO FIND CHEAP FLIGHTS

"The use of travelling is to regulate imagination by reality, and instead of thinking how things may be, to see them as they are." Samuel Jackson

If you're working full-time, you can save yourself a lot of money by requesting your time off from work starting in the middle of the week. Tuesdays and Wednesdays are the cheapest days to fly. You can save thousands just by adjusting your time off.

The simplest secret to booking cheap flights is open parameters. Let's say you want to fly from Chicago to Paris. You enter the USA in from and select France under to. You may find flights from New York City to Paris for $70. Then you just need to find a cheap flight to NYC. Make sure you calculate full costs, including if you need airport accommodation and of course getting to and from airports, **but in nearly every instance open parameters will save you at least half the cost of the flight.**

If you're not sure about where you want to go, use open parameters to show you the cheapest destinations from your city. Start with skyscanner.net they include the low-cost airlines that others like Kayak leave out. Google Flights can also show you cheap destinations. To see these leave the WHERE TO section blank.

Open parameters can also show you the cheapest dates to fly. If you're flexible, you can save up to 80% of the flight cost. Always check the weather at your destination before you book. Sometimes a $400 flight will be $20, because it's monsoon season. But hey, if you like the rain, why not?

ALWAYS USE A PRIVATE BROWSER TO BOOK FLIGHTS

Skyscanner and other sites track your IP address and put prices up and down based on what they determine your strength of conviction to buy. e.g. if you've booked one-way and are looking for the return, these sites will jack the prices up by in most cases 50%. Incognito browsing pays.

Use a VPN such as Hola to book your flight from your destination

Install Hola, change your destination to the country you are flying to. The location from which a ticket is booked can affect the price significantly as algorithms consider local buying power.

Choose the right time to buy your ticket.

Choose the right time to buy your ticket, as purchasing tickets on a Sunday has been proven to be cheaper. If you can only book during the week, try to do it on a Tuesday.

Mistake fares

Email alerts from individual carriers are where you can find the best 'mistake fares". This is where a computer error has resulted in an airline offering the wrong fare. In my experience, it's best to sign up to individual carriers email lists, but if you ARE lazy Secret Flying puts together a daily roster of mistake fares. Visit https://www.secretflying.com/errorfare/ to see if there're any errors that can benefit you.

Fly late for cheaper prices

Red-eye flights, the ones that leave later in the day, are typically cheaper and less crowded, so aim to book that flight if possible. You will also get through the airport much quicker at the end of the day. Just make sure there's ground transport available for when you land. You don't want to save $50 on the airfare and spend it on a taxi to your accommodation.

Use this APP for same day flights

If your plans are flexible, use 'Get The Flight Out' (http://www.gtfoflights.com/) a fare tracker Hopper that shows you same-day deeply discounted flights. This is best for long-haul flights with major carriers. You can often find a British Airways round-trip from JFK Airport to Heathrow for $300. If you booked this in advance, you'd pay at least double.

Take an empty water bottle with you

Airport prices on food and drinks are sky high. It disgusts me to see some airports charging $10 for a bottle of water. ALWAYS take an empty water bottle with you. It's relatively unknown, but most airports have drinking water fountains past the security check. Just type in your airport name to wateratairports.com to locate the fountain. Then once you've passed security (because they don't allow you to take 100ml or more of liquids) you can freely refill your bottle with water.

Round-the-World (RTW) Tickets

It is always cheaper to book your flights using a DIY approach. First, you may decide you want to stay longer in one country, and a RTW will charge you a hefty fee for changing your flight. Secondly, it all depends on where and when you travel and as we have discussed, there are many ways to ensure you pay way less than $1,500 for a year of flights. If you're travelling long-haul, the best strategy is to buy a return ticket, say New York, to Bangkok and then take cheap flights or transport around Asia and even to Australia and beyond.

Cut your costs to and from airports

Don't you hate it when getting to and from the airport is more expensive than your flight! And this is true in so many cities, especially European ones. For some reason, Google often shows the most expensive options. Use Omio to compare the cheapest transport options and save on airport transfer costs.

Car sharing instead of taxis

Check if Norway has car sharing at the airport. Often they'll be tons of cars parked at the airport that are half the price of taking a taxi into the city. In most instances, you register your driving licence on an app and scan the code on the car to get going.

Checking Bags

Sometimes you need to check bags. If you do, put an AirTag inside. That way, you'll be about to see when you land where your bag is. This saves you the nail biting wait at baggage claim. And if worse comes to worst, and you see your bag is actually in another city, you can calmly stroll over to customer services and show them where your bag is.

Is it cheaper and more convenient to send your bags ahead?

Before you check your bags, check if it's cheaper to send them ahead of you with sendmybag.com obviously if you're staying in an Airbnb, you'll need to ask the hosts permission or you can time them to arrive the day after you. Hotels are normally very amenable.

What Credit Card Gives The Best Air Miles?

You can slash the cost of flights just for spending on a piece of plastic.

LET'S TALK ABOUT DEBT

Before we go into the best cards for each country, let's first talk about debt. The US system offers the best and biggest rewards. Why? Because they rely on the fact that many people living in the US will not pay their cards in full and the card will earn the bank significant interest payments. Other countries have a very different attitude towards money, debt, and saving than Americans. Thus in Germany and Austria the offerings aren't as favourable as the UK, Spain and Australia, where debt culture is more widely embraced. The takeaway here is this: **Only spend on one of these cards when you have set-up an automatic total monthly balance repayment. Don't let banks profit from your lizard brain!**

The best air-mile credit cards for those living in the UK

Amex Preferred Rewards Gold comes out top for those living in the UK for 2023.

Here are the benefits:

- 20,000-point bonus on £3,000 spend in first three months. These can be used towards flights with British Airways, Virgin Atlantic, Emirates and Etihad, and often

other rewards, such as hotel stays and car hire.
- 1 point per £1 spent
- 1 point = 1 airline point
- Two free visits a year to airport lounges
- No fee in year one, then £140/yr

The downside:

- Fail to repay fully and it's 59.9% rep APR interest, incl fee

You'll need to cancel before the £140/yr fee kicks in year two if you want to avoid it.

The best air-mile credit cards for those living in Canada

Aeroplan is the superior rewards program in Canada. The card has a high earn rate for Aeroplan Points, generating 1.5 points per $1 spent on eligible purchases. Look at the specifics of the eligible purchases https://www.aircanada.com/ca/en/aco/home/aeroplan/earn.html. If you're not spending on these things AMEX's Membership Rewards program offers you the best returns in Canada.

The best air-mile credit cards for those living in Germany

If you have a German bank account, you can apply for a Lufthansa credit card.

Earn 50,000 award miles if you spend $3,000 in purchases and paying the annual fee, both within the first 90 days.

Earn 2 award miles per $1 spent on ticket purchases directly from Miles & More integrated airline partners.

Earn 1 award mile per $1 spent on all other purchases.

The downsides

the €89 annual fee

Limited to fly with Lufthansa and its partners but you can capitalise on perks like the companion pass and airport lounge vouchers.

You need excellent credit to get this card.

The best air-mile credit cards for those living in Austria

"In Austria, Miles & More offers you a special credit card. You get miles for each purchase with the credit card. The Miles & More program calculates miles earned based on the distance flown and booking class. For European flights, the booking class is a flat rate. For intercontinental flights, mileage is calculated by multiplying the booking class by the distance flown." They offer a calculator so you can see how many points you could earn: https://www.miles-and-more.com/at/en/earn/airlines/mileage-calculator.html

The best air-mile credit cards for those living in Spain:

"The American Express card is the best known and oldest to earn miles, thanks to its membership Rewards program. When making payments with this card, points are added, which can then be exchanged for miles from airlines such as Iberia, Air Europa, Emirates or Alitalia." More information is available here: https://www.americanexpress.com/es-es/

The best air-mile credit cards for those living in Australia

ANZ Rewards Black comes out top for 2023.

180,000 bonus ANZ Reward Points (can get an $800 gift card) and $0 annual fee for the first year with the ANZ Rewards Black
Points Per Spend: 1 Velocity point on purchases of up to

$5,000 per statement period and 0.5 Velocity points there-after.
Annual Fee: $0 in the first year, then $375 after.
Ns no set minimum income required, however, there is a minimum credit limit of $15,000 on this card.

Here are some ways you can hack points onto this card:
https://www.pointhacks.com.au/credit-cards/anz-rewards-black-guide/

The best air-mile credit card solution for those living in the USA with a POOR credit score

The downside to Airline Mile cards is that they require good or excellent credit scores, meaning 690 or higher.

If you have bad credit and want to use credit card air lines you will need to rebuild your credit poor. The Credit One Bank® Platinum Visa® for Rebuilding Credit is a good credit card for people with bad credit who don't want to place a deposit on a secured card. The Credit One Platinum Visa offers a $300 credit limit, rewards, and the potential for credit-limit increases, which in time will help rebuild your score.

PLEASE don't sign-up for any of these cards if you can't trust yourself to repay it in full monthly. This will only lead to stress for you.

Frequent Flyer Memberships

"Points" and "miles" are often used interchangeably, but they're usually two very different things. Maximise and diversify your rewards by utilising both.

A frequent-flyer program (FFP) is a loyalty program offered by an airline. They are designed to encourage airline customers to fly more to accumulate points (also called miles, kilometres, or segments) which can be redeemed for air travel or other rewards.

You can sign up with any FFP program for free. There are three major airline alliances in the world: Oneworld, SkyTeam and Star Alliance. I am with One World https://www.oneworld.com/members because the points can be accrued and used for most flights.

The best return on your points is to use them for international business or first class flights with lie-flat seats. You would need 3 times more miles compared to an economy flight, but if you paid cash, you'd pay 5 - 10 times more than the cost of the economy flight, so it really pays to use your points only for upgrades. The worst value for your miles is to buy an economy seat or worse, a gift from the airlines gift-shop.

Sign up for a family/household account to pool miles together. If you share a common address, you can claim the miles with most airlines. You can use AwardWallet to keep track of your miles. Remember that they only last for 2 years, so use them before they expire.

Relaxing at the Airport

The best way to relax at the airport is in a lounge where they provide free food, drinks, comfortable chairs, luxurious amenities (many have showers) and, if you're lucky, a peaceful ambience. If you're there for a longer time, look for Airport Cubicles, sleep pods which charge by the hour.

You can use your FFP Card (Frequent Flyer Memberships) to get into select lounges for free. Check your eligibility before you pay.

If you're travelling a lot, I'd recommend investing in a Priority Pass for the airport.

It includes 850-plus airport lounges around the world. The cost is $99 for the year and $27 per lounge visit or you can pay $399 for the year all inclusive.

If you need a lounge for a one-off day, you can get a Day Pass. Buy it online for a discount, it always works out cheaper than buying at the airport. Use www.LoungePass.com.

Lounges are also great if you're travelling with kids, as they're normally free for kids and will definitely cost you less than snacks for your little ones. The rule is that kids should be seen and not heard, so consider this before taking an overly excited child who wants to run around, or you might be asked to leave even after you've paid.

How to spend money

Bank ATM fees vary from $2.50 per transaction to as high as $5 or more, depending on the ATM and the country. You can completely skip those fees by paying with card and using a card which can hold multiple currencies.

Budget travel hacking begins with a strategy to spend without fees. Your individual strategy depends on the country you legally reside in as to what cards are available. Happily there are some fin-tech solutions which can save you thousands on those pesky ATM withdrawal fees and are widely available globally. Here are a selection of cards you can pre-charge with currency for Norway:

N26

N26 is a 12-year-old digital bank. I have been using them for over 6 years. The key advantage is fee-free card transactions abroad. They have a very elegant app, where you can check your timeline for all transactions listed in real time or manage your in-app security anywhere. The card you receive is a Mastercard so you can use it everywhere. If you lose the card, you don't have to call anyone, just open the app and swipe 'lock card'. It puts your purchases into a graph automatically so you can see what you spend on. You can open an account from abroad entirely online, all you need is your passport and a camera n26.com

Revolut

Revolut is a multi-currency account that allows you to hold and exchange 29 currencies and spend fee-free abroad. It's a UK based neobank, but accepts customers from all over the world.

Wise debit card

If you're going to be in one place for a long time, the Wise debit card is like having your travel money on a card – it lets you spend money at the real exchange rate.

Monzo

Monzo is good if your UK based. They offer a fee-free UK account. Fee-free international money transfers and fee-free spending abroad.

The downside

The cards above are debit cards, meaning you need to have money in those accounts to spend it. This comes with one big downside: safety. Credit card issuers' have "zero liability" meaning you're not liable for unauthorised charges. All the cards listed above do provide cover for unauthorised charges but times vary greatly in how quickly you'd get your money back if it were stolen.

The best option is to check in your country to see which credit cards are the best for travelling and set up monthly payments to repay the whole amount so you don't pay unnecessary interest. In the USA, Schwab regularly ranks at the top for travel credit cards. Credit cards are always the safer option when abroad simply because you get your money back faster if its stolen and if you're renting cars, most will give you free insurance when you book the car rental using the card, saving you money.

Always withdraw money; never exchange.

Money exchanges, whether they be on the streets or in the airports will NEVER give you a good exchange rate. Do not bring bundles of cash. Instead, withdraw local currency from the ATM as needed and try to use only free ATMs. Many in airports charge you a fee to withdraw cash. Look for bigger ATMs attached to banks to avoid this.

Recap

- Take cash from local, non-charging ATMs for the best rates.

- Never change at airport exchange desks unless you absolutely have to, then just change just enough to be able get to a bank ATM.

- Bring a spare credit card for emergencies.

- Split cash in various places on your person (pockets, shoes) and in your luggage. It's never sensible to keep your cash or cards all in one place.

- In higher risk areas, use a money belt under your clothes or put $50 in your shoe or bra.

Revolut

Revolut is a multi-currency account that allows you to hold and exchange 29 currencies and spend fee-free abroad. It's a UK based neobank, but accepts customers from all over the world.

Wise debit card

If you're going to be in one place for a long time the Wise debit card is like having your travel money on a card – it lets you spend money at the real exchange rate.

Monzo

Monzo is good if your UK based. They offer a fee-free UK account. Fee-free international money transfers and fee-free spending abroad.

The downside

The cards above are debit cards, meaning you need to have money in those accounts to spend it. This comes with one big downside: safety. Credit card issuers' have "zero liability" meaning you're not liable for unauthorised charges. All of the cards listed above do provide cover for unauthorised charges but times vary greatly in how quickly you'd get your money back if it were stolen.

The best option is to check in your country to see which credit cards are the best for travelling and set up monthly payments to repay the whole amount so you don't pay un-necessary interest. In the USA, Schwab[2] regularly ranks at the top for travel credit cards. Credit cards are always the safer option when abroad simply because you get your money back faster if its stolen and if you're renting cars, most will give you free insurance when you book the car rental using the card, saving you money.

---

[2] Charles Schwab High Yield Checking accounts refund every single ATM fee worldwide, require no minimum balance and have no monthly fee.

Always withdraw money; never exchange.

Money exchanges whether they be on the streets or in the airports will NEVER give you a good exchange rate. Do not bring bundles of cash. Instead withdraw local currency from the ATM as needed and try to use only free ATM's. Many in airports charge you a fee to withdraw cash. Look for bigger ATM's attached to banks to avoid this.

Recap

- Take cash from local, non-charging ATMs for the best rates.
- Never change at airport exchange desks unless you absolutely have to, then just change just enough to be able get to a bank ATM.
- Bring a spare credit card for emergencies.
- Split cash in various places on your person (pockets, shoes) and in your luggage. Its never sensible to keep your cash or cards all in one place.
- In higher risk areas, use a money belt under your clothes or put $50 in your shoe or bra.

How to save money while travelling

Saving money while travelling sounds like an oxymoron, but it can be done with little to no effort. Einstein is credited as saying, "Compound interest is the eighth wonder of the world." If you saved and invested $100 today, in 20 years, it would be $2,000 thanks to the power of compound interest. It makes sense then to save your money, invest and make even more money.

The Acorns app is a simple system for this. It rounds up your credit card purchases and puts the rest into a savings account. So if you pay for a coffee and its $3.01, you'll save 0.99 cents. You won't even notice you're saving by using this app: www.acorns.com

Here are some more generic ways you can always save money while travelling:

Device Safety

Having your phone, iPad or laptop stolen is one BIG and annoying way you can lose money travelling. The simple solution is to use apps to track your devices. Some OSes have this feature built-in. Prey will try your smartphones or laptops (preyproject.com).

Book New Airbnb's

When you take a risk on a new Airbnb listing, you save money. Just make sure the hosts profile is at least 3 years old and has reviews.

If you end up in an overcrowded city

The website https://campspace.com/ is like Airbnb for camping in people's garden and is a great way to save money if you end up in a city during a big event.

Look out for free classes

Lots of hostels offer free classes for guests. If you're planning to stay in a hostel, check out what classes your hostel offers. I have learnt languages, cooking techniques, dance styles, drawing and all manner of things for free by taking advantage of free classes at hostels.

Get student discounts

If you're studying buy an ISIC card - International Student Identity Card. It is internationally recognised, valid in 133 countries and offers more than 150,000 discounts!

Get Senior Citizen discounts

Most state run attractions, ie, museums, galleries will offer a discount for people over 65 with ID.

Instal maps.me

Maps me is extremely good for travelling without data. It's like offline google maps without the huge download size.

Always buy travel insurance

Don't travel without travel insurance. It is a small cost to pay compared with what could be a huge medical bill.

Travel Apps That'll Make Budget Travel Easier

Travel apps are useful for booking and managing travel logistics. They have one fatal downside: they can track you in the app and keep prices up. If you face this, access the site from an incognito browser tab.

Here are the best apps and what they can do for you:

- Best For flight Fare-Watching: Hopper.

- Best for booking flights: Skyscanner and Google Flights

- Best for timing airport arrivals: FlightAware - check on delays, cancellations and gate changes.

- Best for overcoming a fear of flying: SkyGuru - turbulence forecasts for the route you're flying.

- Best for sharing your location: TripWhistle - text or send your GPS coordinates or location easily.

- Best for splitting expenses among co-travellers: Splittr, Trip Splitter, Venmo or Splitwise.

How NOT to be ripped off

"One of the great things about travel is that you find out ho w many good, kind people there are."
— Edith Wharton

The quote above may seem ill placed in a chapter entitled how not to be ripped off, but I included it to remind you that the vast majority of people do not want to rip you off. In fact, scammers are normally limited to three situations:

1. Around heavily visited attractions - these places are targeted purposively due to sheer footfall. Many criminals believe ripping people off is simply a numbers game.

2. In cities or countries with low-salaries or communist ideologies. If they can't make money in the country, they seek to scam foreigners. If you have travelled to India, Morocco or Cuba you will have observed this phenomenon.

3. When you are stuck and the person helping you know you have limited options.

Scammers know that most people will avoid confrontation. Don't feel bad about utterly ignoring someone and saying no. Here are six strategies to avoid being ripped off:

1. **Never ever agree to pay as much as you want. Always decide on a price before.**

Whoever you're dealing with is trained to tell you, they are uninterested in money. This is a trap. If you let people do this they will ask for MUCH MORE money at the end, and because you have used there service, you will feel obliged to pay. This is a conman's trick and nothing more.

2. Pack light

You can move faster and easier. If you take heavy luggage, you will end up taking taxis which are comparatively very costly over time.

3. NEVER use the airport taxi service. Plan to use public transport before you reach the airport.

4. Don't buy a sim card from the airport. Buy from the local supermarkets it will cost 50% less.

5. Eat at local restaurants serving regional food

Food defines culture. Exploring all delights available to the palate doesn't need to cost enormous sums.

6. **Ask the locals what something should cost,** and try not to pay over that.

7. **If you find yourself with limited options.** e.g. your taxi dumps you on the side of the road because you refuse to pay more (common in India and parts of South America) don't act desperate and negotiate as if you have other options or you will be extorted.

8. Don't blindly rely on social media[3]

Let's say you post in a Facebook group that you want tips for travelling to The Maldives. A lot of the comments you will receive come from guides, hosts and restaurants doing their own promotion. It's estimated that 50% or more of

---

[3] https://arstechnica.com/tech-policy/2019/12/social-media-plat-forms-leave-95-of-reported-fake-accounts-up-study-finds/

Facebook's current monthly active users are fake. And what's worse, a recent study found Social media platforms leave 95% of reported fake accounts up. These accounts are the digital versions of the men who hang around the Grand Palace in Bangkok telling tourists its closed, to divert you to shops where they will receive a commission for bringing you.

It can also be the case that genuine comments come from people who have totally different interests, beliefs and yes, budgets to yours. Make your experience your own and don't believe every comment you read.

Bottom line: use caution when accepting recommendations on social media and always fact-check with your own research.

Small tweaks on the road add up to big differences in your bank balance

Take advantage of other hotel amenities

If you fancy a swim but you're nowhere near the ocean, try the nearest hotel with a pool. As long as you buy a drink, the hotel staff will probably grant you access.

Fill up your mini bar for free.

Fill up your mini bar for free by storing things from the breakfast bar or grocery shop in your mini bar to give you a greater selection of drinks and food without the hefty price tag.

Save yourself some ironing

Use the steam from the shower to get rid of wrinkles in clothing. If something is creased, leave it trapped with the steam in the bathroom overnight for even better results.

See somewhere else for free

Opt for long stopovers, allowing you to experience another city without spending much money.

Wear your heaviest clothes

On the plane to save weight in your pack, allowing you to bring more with you. Big coats can then be used as pillows to make your flight more comfortable.

Don't get lost while you're away.

Find where you want to go using Google Maps, then type 'OK Maps' into the search bar to store this information for offline viewing.

Use car renting services

Share Now or Car2Go allow you to hire a car for 2 hours for $25 in a lot of European countries.

Share Rides

Use sites like blablacar.com to find others who are driving in your direction. It can be 80% cheaper than normal transport. Just check the drivers reviews.

Use free gym passes

Get a free gym day pass by googling the name of a local gym and free day pass.

When asked by people providing you a service where you are from..

If there's no price list for the service you are asking for, when asked where you are from, Say you are from a lesser-known poorer country. I normally say Macedonia, and if they don't know where it is, add it's a poor country. If you say UK, USA, the majority of Europe bar the well-known poorer countries taxi drivers, tour operators etc will match the price to what they think you pay at home.

Set-up a New Uber/ other car hailing app account for discounts

By googling you can find offers with $50 free for new users in most cities for Uber/ Lyft/ Bolt and alike. Just set up a new gmail.com email account to take advantage.

Where and How to Make Friends

"People don't take trips, trips take people." – John Steinbeck

Become popular at the airport

Want to become popular at the airport? Pack a power bar with multiple outlets and just see how many friends you can make. It's amazing how many people forget their chargers, or who packed them in the luggage that they checked in.

Stay in Hostels

First of all, Hostels don't have to be shared dorms, and they cater to a much wider demographic than is assumed. Hostels are a better environment for meeting people than hotels, and more importantly, they tended to open up excursion opportunities that further opened up that opportunity.

Or take up a hobby

If hostels are a definite no-no for you; find an interest. Take up a hobby where you will meet people. I've dived for years and the nature of diving is you're always paired up with a dive buddy. I met a lot of interesting people that way.

Small tweaks on the road add up to big differences in your bank balance

Take advantage of other hotel's amenities

If you fancy a swim but you're nowhere near the ocean, try the nearest hotel with a pool. As long as you buy a drink, the hotel staff will likely grant you access.

Fill up your mini bar for free.

Fill up your mini bar for free by storing things from the breakfast bar or grocery shop in your mini bar to give you a greater selection of drinks and food without the hefty price tag.

Save yourself some ironing

Use the steam from the shower to get rid of wrinkles in clothing. If something is creased, leave it trapped with the steam in the bathroom overnight for even better results.

See somewhere else for free

Opt for long stopovers, allowing you to experience another city without spending much money.

Wear your heaviest clothes

on the plane to save weight in your pack, allowing you to bring more with you. Big coats can then be used as pillows to make your flight more comfortable.

Don't get lost while you're away.

Find where you want to go using Google Maps, then type 'OK Maps' into the search bar to store this information for offline viewing.

Use car renting services

Share Now or Car2Go allow you to hire a car for 2 hours for $25 in a lot of Europe.

Share Rides

Use sites like blablacar.com to find others who are driving in your direction. It can be 80% cheaper than normal transport. Just check the drivers reviews.

Use free gym passes

Get a free gym day pass by googling the name of a local gym and free day pass.

When asked by people providing you a service where you are from..

If there's no price list for the service you are asking for, when asked where you are from, Say you are from a lesser-known poorer country. I normally say Macedonia, and if they don't know where it is, add it's a poor country. If you say UK, USA, the majority of Europe bar the well-known poorer countries taxi drivers, tour operators etc will match the price to what they think you pay at home.

Set-up a New Uber/ other car hailing app account for discounts

By googling you can find offers with $50 free for new users in most cities for Uber/ Lyft/ Bolt and alike. Just set up a new gmail.com email account to take advantage.

Hacks for Families

Rent an Airbnb apartment so you can cook

Apartments are much better for families, as you have all the amenities you'd have at home. They are normally cheaper per person too. We are the first travel guide publisher to include Airbnb's in our recommendations if you think any of these need updating you can email me at philgtang@gmail.com

Shop at local markets

Eat seasonal products and local products. Get closer to the local market and observe the prices and the offer. What you can find more easily, will be the cheapest.

Take Free Tours

Download free podcast tours of the destination you are visiting. The podcast will tell you where to start, where to go, and what to look for. Often you can find multiple podcast tours of the same place. Listen to all of them if you like, each one will tell you a little something new.

Pack Extra Ear Phones

If you go on a museum tour, they often have audio guides. Instead of having to rent one for each person, take some extra earphones. Most audio tour devices have a place to plug in a second set.

Buy Souvenirs Ahead of Time

If you are buying souvenirs somewhere touristy, you are paying a premium price. By ordering the same exact products online, you can save a lot of money.

Use Cheap Transportation

Do as the locals do, including weekly passes.

Carry Reusable Water Bottles

Spending money on water and other beverages can quickly add up. Instead of paying for drinks, take some refillable water bottles.

Combine Attractions

Many major cities offer ticket bundles where one price gets you into 5 or 6 popular attractions. You will need to plan ahead of time to decide what things you plan to do on vacation and see if they are selling these activities together.

Pack Snacks

Granola bars, apples, baby carrots, bananas, cheese crackers, juice boxes, pretzels, fruit snacks, apple sauce, grapes, and veggie chips.

Stick to Carry-On Bags

Do not pay to check a large bag. Even a small child can pull a carry-on.

Visit free art galleries and museums

Just google the name + free days.

Eat Street Food

There's a lot of unnecessary fear around this. You can watch the food prepared. Go for the stands that have a steady queue.

Travel Gadgets for Families

Dropcam

Are what-if scenarios playing out in your head? Then you need Dropcam.

'Dropcam HD Internet Wi-Fi Video Monitoring Cameras help you watch what you love from anywhere. In less than a minute, you'll have it setup and securely streaming video to you over your home Wi-Fi. Watch what you love while away with Dropcam HD.'

Approximate Price: $139

Kelty-Child-Carrier

Voted as one of the best hiking essentials if you're traveling with kids and can carry a child up to 18kg.

Jetkids Bedbox

No more giving up your own personal space on the plane with this suitcase that becomes a bed.

How I got hooked on budget travelling

'We're on holiday' is what my dad used to say to justify getting us in so much debt we lost our home and all our things when I was 11. We moved from the suburban bliss of Hemel Hempstead to a run down council estate in inner-city London, near my dad's new job as a refuge collector, a fancy word for dustbin man. I lost all my school friends while watching my dad go through a nervous breakdown.

My dad loved walking up a hotel lobby desk without a care in the world. So much so, that he booked overpriced holidays on credit cards. A lot of holidays. As it turned out, we couldn't afford any of them. In the end, my dad had no choice but to declare bankruptcy. When my mum realised, he'd racked up so much debt our family unit dissolved. A neat and perhaps as painless a summary of events that lead me to my life's passion: budget travel that doesn't compromise on fun, safety or comfort.

I started travelling full-time at the age of 18. I wrote the first Super Cheap Insider guide for friends visiting Norway - which I did for a month on less than $250. When sales reached 10,000 I decided to form the Super Cheap Insider Guides company. As I know from first-hand experience debt can be a noose around our necks, and saying 'oh come on, we're on vacation' isn't a get out of jail free card. In fact, its the reverse of what travel is supposed to bring you - freedom.

Before I embarked upon writing Super Cheap Insider guides, many, many people told me that my dream was impossible. Travelling on a budget could never be comfortable. I hope this guide has proved to you what I have known for a long-time: budget travel can feel luxurious when you know and use the insider hacks.

And apologies if I depressed you with my tale of woe. My dad is now happily remarried and works as a chef in London at a fancy hotel - the kind he used to take us to!

A final word...

There's a simple system you can use to think about budget travel. In life, we can choose two of the following: cheap, fast, or quality. So if you want it Cheap and fast you will get a lower quality service. Fast-food is the perfect example. The system holds true for purchasing anything while travelling. I always choose cheap and quality, except at times where I am really limited on time. Normally, you can make small tweaks to make this work for you. Ultimately, you must make choices about what's most important to you and heed your heart's desires.

'Your heart is the most powerful muscle in your body. Do what it says.' Jen Sincero

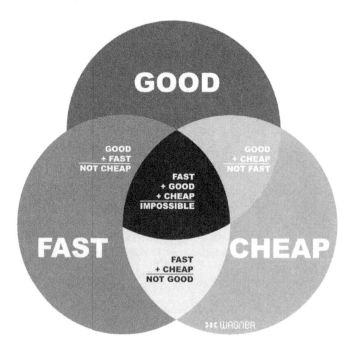

If you've found this book useful, please select five stars on Amazon. Knowing I helped you save money in Norway would mean genuinely make my day.

Copyright

Published in Great Britain in 2023 by Super Cheap Insider Guides LTD.

Copyright © 2023 Super Cheap Insider Guides LTD.

The right of Phil G A Tang to be identified as the Author of the Work has been asserted in accordance with the Copyright, Designs and Patents Act 1988.